What People Are Saying About

Thread of Life

I started reading your book yesterday morning and finished it this afternoon! I found it fascinating. It is a fine work ... The book is rich in social observation. I shall long cherish your reflections on memory and history.

Harvey Gillman, author of *A Light That Is Shining*, *A Minority of One*, and *Epiphanies*

Sober and sobering, Jennifer Kavanagh's Thread of Life is a thoughtful, serious work of remembrance. The memoir's canvas is large, embracing multiple themes — music, Jewishness, mothers, home and place — as well as historical context both micro and macro. A widely researched work, it considers family fortunes, some tragic, with devotion and also detachment.

Elsbeth Lindner, former CEO of The Women's Press and author of *The Meeting*

I have always been convinced that memoirs, true stories, are more fascinating and enthralling than fiction books. The story of two ladies, mother and daughter, their lives in Russia, Latvia, Switzerland, Egypt and England in the 20th century absorbed me into this page-turner brilliantly written by Jennifer Kavanagh, their granddaughter and daughter respectively. I could not stop from following the threads of many lives until I got to the last page of the book and exclaimed: спасибо [thank you] — it is a fascinating book. I regret I could not listen to that lullaby in Russian that Dora had sung to Genia.

Sergei Nikitin, author of *Friends ar*

T0343139

Books by Jennifer Kavanagh

The Methuen Book of Animal Tales (ed.) 9780416247602
The Methuen Book of Humorous Stories (ed.) 9780416506105
Call of the Bell Bird 9780852453650
The World Is Our Cloister 9781846940491
New Light (ed.) 9781846941436
Journey Home (formerly The O of Home) 9781780991511
Simplicity Made Easy 9781846945434
Small Change, Big Deal 9781780993133
The Failure of Success 9789781780998
A Little Book of Unknowing 9781782798088
Heart of Oneness 9781785356858
Practical Mystics 9781789042795
Let Me Take You by the Hand 9781408713143
Do Quakers Pray? 9781803414003

Fiction

The Emancipation of B 9781782798
The Silence Diaries 9781789041828
And this shall be my dancing day 9781803412450

Thread of Life

My Russian legacy

Thread of Life

My Russian legacy

by Jennifer Kavanagh

London, UK
Washington, DC, USA

CollectiveInk

First published by Liberalis Books, 2025
Liberalis Books is an imprint of Collective Ink Ltd.,
Unit 11, Shepperton House, 89 Shepperton Road, London, N1 3DF
office@collectiveinkbooks.com
www.collectiveinkbooks.com
www.liberalisbooks.com

For distributor details and how to order please visit the 'Ordering' section on our website.

Text copyright: Jennifer Kavanagh 2024

ISBN: 978 1 80341 800 1
978 1 80341 808 7 (ebook)
Library of Congress Control Number: 2024932952

All rights reserved. Reproduction or translation of any part of this book through any means
without permission of the copyright owner is unlawful, except for promotional use. Request for
other permissions or further information should be addressed in writing to the author.

The rights of Jennifer Kavanagh as author have been asserted in accordance with the Copyright,
Designs and Patents Act 1988.

A CIP catalogue record for this book is available from the British Library.

Design: Lapiz Digital Services

UK: Printed and bound by CPI Group (UK) Ltd, Croydon, CR0 4YY
Printed in North America by CPI GPS partners

This book is not intended as a substitute for professional medical advice. The reader should
consult the appropriate healthcare professional regarding specific needs. All client names used
herein are pseudonyms to protect privacy.

We operate a distinctive and ethical publishing philosophy in
all areas of our business, from our global network of authors to
production and worldwide distribution.

For Sophie, who was born just as the idea for this began to form.

I ka wā ma mua, ka wā ma hope. (Hawaian)
We're walking backward into the future.

If you look deeply into the palm of your hand you will see your parents and all generations of your ancestors. All of them are alive in this moment. Each is present in your body. You are the continuation of each of those people ... The thread of life has never been interrupted from time without beginning until now. Previous generations ... are present in your hand at this moment. (Thich Nhat Hanh, *Present Moment, Wonderful Moment.* Berkeley, California: Parallax Press, 1990. pp 13–14.)

Contents

Acknowledgements

Thanks, most of all, to my brother, Eric Weil, whose remarkable memory has enriched this book. Also thanks to, among others, Sean Bye, Frank Crampton, Peter Daniels, Poury Fischberg, Scheherazade Fischberg, Harvey Gillman, Jo Hines, Geoffrey Hosking, David Irwin, Margrieta Langins, Charles Lee, Alastair McIntosh, Sergei Nikitin, Maggy Whitehouse

References in the text are to entries in Further Reading at the end of the book.

Preface

September 2022, Regent's Park, London

It was time for the annual open-air sculpture exhibition. I stood in front of one exhibit: a panel inscribed in large letters with "Some unnecessary words", and chuckled.

"Funny," I said to the young woman standing next to me.

But she didn't understand. She was from Ukraine, and she spoke Russian.

With her few words of English and my few words remembered from school Russian, we managed to communicate. I told her that my mother was Russian, my grandfather (probably) from Ukraine.

Her face lit up. "Town?"

But I didn't know — we've never known.

She told me she talks to her mother on the phone, and scrolled down her phone past pictures of Putin to show a picture of an explosion.

My hand on my heart, I expressed my sorrow.

We gazed at each other then, realising we had said all that was possible, we said goodbye. She opened her arms and embraced me.

Six months before this meeting, and a few months after I started work on this book, the Russian army invaded Ukraine. The day after the invasion, behind me as I walked along a London street, were two young women talking Russian. Not an easy time to be Russian; not a time, indeed, where I feel comfortable admitting my Russian ancestry. But thousands of Russians in many Russian cities are protesting against the war, and being arrested. Courage, indeed. Reminders of Prague in 1968 when the Soviet tanks rolled in — and of the courage of many other protestors. Warmongering governments are not always supported by their citizens. Nonetheless, it gave me pause, and I stopped working on the book for a while, to be clearer about the context in which I was writing.

Threads

Margate, February 2022. An unexpectedly balmy day by the sea. I was there with a friend to visit the Turner Contemporary Gallery, where her daughter was exhibiting two pieces of artwork. It was a large exhibition, full of paintings and other art of varying quality. Suddenly, as I wandered through the rooms, I was arrested by an artwork by Barbarita Marks called "Threads". Two Singer sewing machines. A piece of cloth with large stitches linking printed portraits of a Jewish grandmother, and those of her daughter and granddaughters. The artist writes:

> This installation searches for connection. My mother, Bina Korngold fled from Vienna in 1939, to escape the Nazis. As soon as she was able to speak English, she gave up speaking German forever as a private stand against the killing of her parents Markus and Bruche Korngold.
>
> Threads uses the politics of repair, stitching time, placing images of our mother, my sister, Gita and I, close to those of our lost Viennese grandparents.

Different names, different nationalities, but it was a visible representation of the theme of this book. An extraordinary piece of synchronicity that I take to be significant.

Part I
Dora and Genia

Introduction

Whether called faith, destiny, or the hand of God,
slender threads are at work bringing coherence and
continuity to our lives. Over time they weave a
remarkable tapestry.
(Robert A. Johnson, quoted in Anders).

When I interviewed my mother, she was in her mid-nineties. She was old. What she saw, heard, remembered, was patchy; like her failing macula, the centre of the picture was sometimes a black hole. Not "sans teeth, sans eyes, sans taste, sans everything" but getting that way. I too am growing old. But I am determined to fill in that black hole, to reclaim what can be found of my past, the generations that went to inform, to form, my life. Through genes and memory we are one with those who have gone before, and those who are to come. Indigenous cultures have long pointed the way to what some would consider our responsibility to the legacy of our forebears. The truth, the reality, of my ancestors' lives, which have gone on to inform mine, has been revealed over a long lifetime, in fits and starts, in vivid scenes, filling in just one corner of the whole jigsaw. When I have been ready to see them.

Genealogy has traditionally been traced in the male line: the women's stories are often lost. Jewish identity is matrilinear: it passes through the female line, so it would seem entirely appropriate that the tracing of the threads in this Jewish story be largely through the women. Three generations of women: my grandmother, my mother, and myself. Many others will appear, but I have not wanted to take the story into the next, living, generation. Their stories will be their own. This is about two Russian women: Dora and her daughter, Evgenia

(Genia), whose lives spanned the period from the end of the nineteenth century till the second decade of the twenty-first, and encompassed wars and revolution, capture and escape, the Holocaust. And their legacy to me.

This is a story not just of a family but of a momentous century, seen through the prism of their lives, in Russia, Latvia, Switzerland, Egypt and England. War and peace. But both the century and their individual lives also brought beauty and music, romantic tales and devotion. This is a story with gaps: gaps in time, gaps in knowledge and, no doubt, in understanding. There are holes where facts should be, and even in factual accounts there is a lack of consistency in the versions told of the same events. Even the "facts" often seem to lack certainty When the factual information is lacking, conjecture has to take its place.

History and Memory

The former chief rabbi of the UK, Jonathan Sacks, has written often on this subject:

> There is a profound difference between history and memory. History is His Story — an event that happened sometime else to someone else. Memory is my story — something that happened to me and is part of who I am.

And again:

> Memory is about identity. It is the story of which I am a part. That story may be ancient. In the case of Passover it is very ancient indeed. But I am part of it. That is what identity is — being part of a continuing narrative, one of whose characters I am. History answers the question, "What happened?" Memory answers the question, "Who am I?"

Memory is my story, the past that made me who I am, of whose legacy I am the guardian for the sake of generations yet to come. Without memory, there is no identity, and without identity, we are mere dust on the surface of infinity.
https://www.rabbisacks.org/archive

As well as History and Memory, maybe we need to consider My Story and Her Story.

Commenting on these pieces by Sacks, Maggy Whitehouse, an independent practising minister and specialist in Judaeo-Christian mysticism, says: "I'd add that Her Story is frequently referred to as Heresy — which, in the original Greek was a neutral term that signified merely the holding of a particular set of philosophical opinions. It only later came to be interpreted as 'opposition to Church doctrine'. My Story transformed through healing is 'Mystery' unless we let it degenerate into 'My-Sob-Story' which is when we embrace 'woundology' — the adopting of unhappiness or dis-ease as part of our identity."

This book brings the interweaving of history and memory, the general and the particular, the global with the tiny details of family life, the sweep of the overview and the focus of the microscope. To some extent, that must be true of all biographies, but is perhaps especially so when historical events are brought into such sharp focus by what is happening in the present moment. To view this broader perspective, we need to don varifocal lenses. There will be some History — necessary facts to set the context but the bulk will be Her Story, with a more personal, intuitive and spiritual dimension: one that is largely told through the stories of the women. This is the oral tradition of history, fluid enough to update with every generation. Most of all, there is Memory: My Story and a part of who I am. I was not brought up a Jew, so find I am only now learning the deeper truths of what it means to be one.

* * *

At the heart of this book is the figure of Dora, Dorotea, "gift of God", my maternal grandmother. My mother spoke about her often, and said that not a day passed when she did not think of Dora, and pray for her, for Dora's brother, her beloved uncle Sasha, and their mother.

> I remember my mother, who was slender and elegant, and she always used to have a flower stuck in her waist. In her very tiny waist. I wish you could have known her: she loved music, literature and was such a gentle person.

And that is how Dora appears in the tiny gold-framed photo that I have: a Chekhovian figure in a long white dress, a flower at her wasp waist, a broad-brimmed hat. I never met her, but, through my mother's memories and heart-felt love, in some sense, I feel I know her. Dora has always been a presence in my life.

My mother too was elegant — and very beautiful, with pale skin and long very dark hair. When she was young she wore it in plaits or in waves down her back. Later, she boasted that in her youth her hair was so long that she could sit on it. A large studio photo taken in the 1940s, when my mother was twenty-seven, and displayed for many years in a silver frame in my parents' London sitting room, shows a classic beauty, highlighted in a fashionable, and becoming, half shadow.

By the time she was forty, that dark hair had become a very dramatic white — a family trait that we have all to some degree inherited. My mother was always elegant, chic, even into old age, wearing sheer stockings, rings on her slender fingers, and a touch of lipstick.

Dora was both a romantic presence and the cause of a terrible sadness that cast a cloud over my mother and our family life. Fifty-seven years alive; seventy-five a shadow. Writing this book is both to mark Dora's fate and to celebrate her life. And to trace the threads from her to my mother, and to myself, with a forward glance to my granddaughter, Sophie, born as I began to think about this book, in 2020. This book is dedicated to her.

I've lived a privileged life. Unlike my mother and grandmother, whose lives were beset with revolution, war, acute danger, narrow escapes, exile, and the Holocaust, I've never been faced with danger, never lived through a war.

My father's family — at least on the male line — is well documented, right back to the Huguenots at the beginning of the eighteenth century. Not so, my mother's. We know only a little from what she told us, and from a plethora of often unidentifiable photos, letters in several languages, and a few written records. So we are largely reliant on my mother's memories, and those of the people she entrusted them to. My own is faulty; I was hoping to mine the longer memory of my aunt and that of my cousin, but they both said that my mother's brother, my uncle Michaïl (Mischa), barely spoke of his mother. Fortunately, my brother Eric, who is eight years older than me, is blessed with a good memory, both of what my mother told him and also of his own childhood in the Second World War.

So, what we learn of this story is seen through the veil of others' memories, a shifting veil revealing different aspects as it blows in the wind — sometimes different versions of the same event. The same story told by different people in different ways, some of which only emerged in the writing of the book. We are reliant on what and whose stories we choose to remember. The stories we want to tell and to hear. We give our lives form in the way we choose to remember them.

In 2021 I published a book called *Let Me Take You by the Hand*, an oral history of London's streets, interviewing and giving voice to some hundreds of people living or working on the streets. Someone asked me: "How do you know if they are telling the truth?" My answer was that I didn't but that like the rest of us, they have found ways of telling their stories that they can live with. The same can be said of what I've been told for this book. As Ariadne Oliver told Hercule Poirot in one of their investigations:

> The trouble is when you remember things you don't always remember them right, do you? ... When people remember something and tell you about it — I mean it's not quite actually what occurred, but it's what they themselves thought occurred (Christie, 145–46).

My mother used to call herself a citizen of the world, a term which has in some UK quarters recently become a term of disparagement. But, if anyone had the right to that description, it was she. Born in St Petersburg, Russia, she lived there till the age of five, when they moved to Riga in Latvia and, after two years, to Chur, near Zurich in Switzerland, where she did most of her growing up. After a year at the Sorbonne in Paris, she came back to Switzerland where she met and married a Swiss, Felix, and they moved to Cairo, Egypt. After his death in 1941, she met my English father, married him, and came finally to England in 1945. All that by the age of thirty. And, apart from a year in Malaysia, it was in England that she lived until her death, over seventy years later.

We recorded the interview in 2010 in the sitting room of my mother's London home, a house I grew up in and one she had lived in for over sixty years. That represented a stability that was at odds with the earlier part of her life, which is what we were going to talk about. My mother was born in 1915: during the First World War and in the uneasy period two years before the outbreak of the Russian Revolution. In the interview, we sadly only got as far as about 1922, when she was seven years old, and when she and some of her family arrived in Switzerland, but at least we have some record of her earliest years in Russia and in Riga — or at least what she remembered at the age of

95, or remembered being told. It seems common for people as they age to remember events in their childhood as if there is some concertinaing of memory from the beginning to the end of life. It was indeed extraordinary what she could remember, in a patchy way — sometimes the smallest, most inconsequential matters. For instance, apparently, her father Dmitri liked to wear tight trousers and would get his batman or aide-de-camp to hold them open while he climbed onto a settee and jumped into them.

But my mother barely mentioned her father in the interview, or at any time. She knew little of him: she didn't even know where he was born. She told me that he had a little property in Ukraine, which was part of the Russian Empire at the time. "I don't know if he was from there, or from St Petersburg." There are many Fischbergs in Ukraine, so he could very well have come from there. In the interview, my mother said she thought he had bought the land, but a previous version told to my brother was that he had been gifted it by the Tzar, for services rendered.

And sometimes her memory was faulty, or at least partial. For instance, when I asked her, *Were you able to take much with you?* her answer was "Nothing. And my mother never got anything back: her lovely piano, beautiful furniture, everything."

That wasn't quite true. My uncle Mischa had silver from their Russian life, as did we — a samovar that I remember being in our dining room, though I think my mother later gave it to a friend. And heavy silver cutlery that we think may have been from Dora's or even her mother's dowry, and that my brother is using to this day. We also had a Russian silver tea service, which disappeared from our London home.

And my mother would tell different people different versions of events. The disappearance of the silver tea set was a case in point: to my daughter, she said she had sold it when times were hard, but my brother remembers clearly the burglary at our

London home when it was stolen. As Queen Elizabeth said of her family conversations, "recollections may vary". There's a certain competitiveness about what each has been told. It seems important for each of us that we were told the right version. We have the truth. But as increasingly becomes clear, memory is unreliable, and truth elusive. As a friend said, every bit of family folklore probably holds a grain of truth.

Pictures may be worth a thousand words, but that worth is reliant on context. So many of the hundreds of photos that we inherited when my mother died meant little to us. As we went through the old albums, we saw gatherings of friends and portraits of stately middle-aged or elderly gentlemen, presumably relatives — but who were they? My aunt and cousin have photos too, and have no idea whom they depict. Pictures can tell a story, yes, but are not always properly interpreted. My brother sent me a copy of himself as a baby with Dora, who died when he was two — I had not known such a picture existed or even that they had met, and wondered when and where it could have been taken. In Riga? It's possible. There was a historic visit to Riga when Eric was a baby; maybe then. But my aunt swears that the picture is not of Dora, but of Dora's sister Becca. Who can tell?

A Rose by any other name

Changes of name have been commonplace throughout history, and often make tracing family difficult. My mother was named Evgenia at birth; in the French-speaking days of her first marriage, she was Eugenie. In England, she became Eugenia — not a version she ever liked.

Dora was short for Dorotea. I am named for her: Dorothy, again a less attractive English version, is my middle name. My brother Eric's middle name also reflects our parentage — Bernard for our devoutly Jewish great-grandfather.

After my mother's death, we discovered that my grandfather was Jewish too, his original name was Schmul Moshe, or as it is listed in the Hall of Names in Yad Vashem, Dmitrijs Zāmuels Fisberga. Like many in an antisemitic country, he changed his name to fit in with local names. Eric also changed his name — in this case his surname. His name at birth was his father's — Weil — and he used it until he was about nine or ten then used his stepfather's name. When, in 1965, his son was due to be born he felt that the original family name would be more appropriate.

Jerusalem, 1994: The first tug of the thread

In 1994 I went with friends to Israel. My visit to Jerusalem was one that I made alone, as a pilgrimage to what felt to me at that time a holy city, a symbol of the unity of faiths that was becoming central to my own. As so often, my expectations were dashed. I stayed in the Christian quarter of the old city and learned for the first time the extent of the oppression of the Palestinian people, which put into perspective the golden view of Israel with which I'd grown up. The Dome of the Rock and the Al-Aqsa mosque retained an air of sanctity, but much of the city, thronged with tourists, left me cold, and the primary Christian church, the Holy Sepulchre, was for me spiritually void.

To my surprise, it was at the Western (Wailing) Wall that I was forcibly struck, knocked off balance, by grief for Dora, the grandmother I'd never known, and her terrible death. As I saw throngs of people standing, kneeling, praying, and the messages tucked into the crevices of the wall, I found myself praying for her. It was the first time that I felt in my heart the tug of that ancestral thread.

The pain of my grandmother's death was a constant undercurrent of my childhood, held in my mother's heart, though never discussed. The Holocaust threw a dark shadow on our lives. It's something I've avoided all my life — I would never read about it, or see a film that dealt with it — till now. It's taken me all this time to face what it's meant in the life of my family.

St Petersburg (Petrograd), 1915–20

In March 2022, a month after Russia's invasion of Ukraine, Alan Little of BBC News gave a valuable insight into Russia and its history. He says he remembers meeting a driver

> who could remember, as a boy, seeing German troops on the outskirts of Moscow in the 1940s ... "This is how close they came, the Germans."
>
> Napoleon's army had gone further the previous century. That experience — that chronic sense of an insecure western frontier — informs the way Russian leaders have thought about their "near abroad".
>
> The Russian emblem, the double-headed eagle, looks both east and west. History has pulled Russia in opposing directions — democratic nation statehood in one direction, domineering imperial power in the other.

(The double-headed eagle has been used as a motif in many countries, and also by some British families. By an extraordinary coincidence, it is the crest of my father's family, to be found on the ex libris bookplates in my grandfather's books.)

Go to St Petersburg and you will see another aspect of this dual character. It is the country's beautiful bay window on the Gulf of Finland. It is an 18th Century city, facing west. It is the European Enlightenment in architectural form. Under the Tsars it was the imperial capital.

After the Russian Revolution of 1917, the Bolsheviks moved the capital back to Moscow and power retreated behind the high, crenelated walls of the Kremlin. It is the architecture of defensiveness, of suspicion, even fear.

When Russian leaders look west from here, they see flat open countryside rolling away to the south and west for hundreds of miles. There are no natural frontiers.

As Alan Little implies, in 2022, that defensive attitude was reinforced. With the invasion of Ukraine came separation from Europe and an emphasis on the non-European aspect of Russia. In its wish to cut off Ukraine's access to the Black Sea and as other countries supported the Ukrainian cause and imposed sanctions, Russia in fact became more isolated.

* * *

Emperor Peter the Great designed and built St Petersburg in 1703 to make Russia feel like a part of Europe. Out of marshland, he created a beautiful Russian city, with a network of canals and glorious palaces akin to Amsterdam and Venice. Peter hired skilled workers and experts from all over Europe: engineers, architects, shipbuilders, scientists, and businessmen. The large number of educated professionals who moved in rendered St Petersburg a much more cosmopolitan city than Moscow and the rest of Russia. Thus Peter created an imperial capital with a European face: a place where many world-known writers, musicians, and artists, as well as architects and scientists, lived and worked. A city of extremes, but also with a middle class with a strong cultural tradition. And it was in that Europe-facing city, that cultural centre, that my mother was born, and to which she felt allegiance.

But there are downsides. St Petersburg is a beautiful city, yes, but also unhealthy. Built on marshland and with poor sanitation, the summers are variable and the winters cold. In pre-Revolutionary days those who could afford to left in for more comfortable climes. With its good European connections, it was easy to escape.

The beauty of the city was also achieved at a terrible price: built on the back of the thousands of conscripts, convicts, and prisoners of war who had been dragooned to build it. "Living in ramshackle quarters and working with inadequate tools — often digging by hand and carrying the dirt in the front of their shirts — these involuntary labourers died in their thousands, carried off by disease or frequent flooding" (the *Guardian*, March 23, 2016). So the very origins of the city were rooted in an inequality that bore the seeds of revolution.

St Petersburg has twice changed its name. In 1914, at the beginning of the First World War, as a reaction to the Germanic sound of its name, the name was changed to Petrograd and then in 1924 it was again changed to Leningrad, reverting to its original name in 1991. From 1713 to 1918 St Petersburg served as the capital of the Tsardom of Russia and the subsequent Russian Empire. After the October Revolution in 1917, the Bolsheviks moved their government to Moscow. At the time of my mother's birth in 1915, it was called Petrograd, though she always referred to it as St Petersburg, and I have decided to follow that practice here.

At this time, the central part of the city was home to many professionals, including my mother's family. Our knowledge of their lives in those early days is very patchy. My mother talked of her family, but we know nothing about their friends or the community in which they lived. Although she remembered an extraordinary amount of her early childhood, unsurprisingly my mother's memories of that turbulent time were mostly domestic — "I remember having a nanny and a black dog." The picture she painted was of a very privileged life. The family had two flats: one for the summer, which was cool, one for the winter which was warm, both in St Petersburg and, like many other affluent families, sometimes in the summer they left the city to go somewhere with a better climate — in their case to a place near a lake in Finland. Of their main St Petersburg flat, my mother said:

The flat was large, I think it was probably on one floor. No garden. We had steps to a gallery. I don't remember the street, but it was near Nevsky Prospect, so quite a smart area. My mother was very elegant, I remember that. I spent a lot of time with my nanny — she always used to come … I remember the white nights, because my mother couldn't sleep, and she used to sit in the nursery by the window and read when we had a nanny. In Russian, yes. Yes, she spoke French and German. Everybody in my family — *interrupted by phone* —

I don't remember what I was saying. But I was read stories, and listened to music — well one of the first ones, with records. And I can still remember one of the songs. No, I can't sing. *Instead, she recites it in Russian.*

Yes, my mother sang me songs.

How many people lived in the flat?

Well, my father, my mother, myself, my brother — oh, and I think that Sasha, my uncle — my mother's brother — lived with us at one stage. He was an engineer. A little older than my mother, two years. I think. My father had an office, he bought — what are they called? He was a chemist. They are registered. Patents, yes, he had some, [according to my brother Eric, paid for with Dora's money] he bought some, he made a lot of money. He was a pharmacist. He was in his thirties, they both were. And [her cousin] Berthe came to see us when she lived there. Her mother lived there — Aunt Ada, and my uncle —

he was a womaniser — and there was Berthe's brother, I can't remember him.

Even in those uncertain times, even in the harsh winter weather, they went out. My mother used to talk about the intense cold; how in the winter the temperature sometimes dropped to −40 degrees, and they would run from one doorway to another to prevent their noses being frozen off! One of my mother's strongest memories was of horse-drawn coaches.

It made such a strong impression. The horses sometimes fell on the ice. No, the carriage didn't belong to the family. I was terribly upset because they whipped the horses. I was very nervous to go in the sledge — it was a sledge — because I was so afraid of the horses falling. Yes, a coachman.

She would have been even more upset to hear that some people waited for fallen horses to die, so that they could carve them up for food. She was not alone in her distress. The Russian Countess Edith Sollohub, who wrote about her life in revolutionary Russia, describes how she was unable to escape the turmoil of St Petersburg, but not only found a way of earning a living but made it her mission to help fallen horses to their feet.

Revolution

At the time of my mother's birth, Russia was plunged into the First World War; it was also building up to the revolution that came to a head two years later. The Russian Revolution was one of the most explosive political events of the twentieth century. With an initial stage in February 1917 before the Bolshevik Revolution in October of that year, it marked the end of centuries of tsarist rule. Initially prompted by food shortages, overcrowded living conditions in the cities, and catastrophic Russian losses during the First World War, the root causes can be traced to the long-standing economic hardship and deep-rooted inequalities in the country as a whole. Eighty-five percent of the population at the time was made up of rural peasants, serfs, in thrall to what amounted to a feudal state. The contrast between the luxury of the imperial court and nobles' palaces and the poverty of the working classes was extreme. Around the turn of the twentieth century, as industrialisation drew increasing numbers of peasants to the capital to work in factories, the situation grew to a crisis point.

And during the First World War, as demand for ever more soldiers increased, the peasant population grew angry as young men and horses, both essential for the war, were taken away, reducing the amount they could grow and damaging their already precarious standard of living. Using the slogan "Bread, Peace and Land", the Bolsheviks opposed any further involvement in the First World War, and supported the transfer of land from the landowners to the peasants. The Revolution pitted peasants against landowners, soldiers against officers, workers against employers, and the general populace, including poor industrial workers, against anyone seemingly with power or money.

In March 1917 there were food riots in St Petersburg; the army was ineffective and, in the end, the Tsar was forced to abdicate. The poet Nina Berberova was in her last year of school, and caught up, like her peers, with the mass protests. "Protest was our environment and my first strong feeling" (7). She later wrote:

Today the swiftness with which Russia collapsed ... seems to me a kind of fantasy. In the upper classes people simply threw everything away and fled: first the tsar and the ministers, then the members of the K.D. Party [the

Constitutional Democratic Party], then the socialists. The least competent and stupidest remained, till they too tumbled into the depths of nothingness. (78)

Until the second and decisive phase of the Revolution later in the year, life was increasingly precarious. However, even as food became scarcer and more expensive, in an extraordinary way the cultural life of the city continued. According to the historian A.J.P. Taylor, "most people did not even know that a revolution was happening. The trams were running, the fashionable restaurants were crowded, the theatre was crowded" (Reed, xvi). The newspapers had been so full of forecasts of a bloody insurrection, of action by armed soldiers, that people didn't notice that an uprising — a quiet and nonviolent seizure of power — was actually taking place.

But with the October Revolution began a civil war that lasted for several years and killed millions of Russians. During this time, life in St Petersburg was unstable and dangerous, with serious hunger and the prospect of sudden violence. Mary McAuley quotes a visitor to the city in 1919 as referring to it as "a silent city" and to its "deathly whiteness" as mountains of snow were left uncleared. Street lighting was turned off, and the dark streets were full of dangers of thieving and attack. McAuley paints a vivid picture of the devastations of the city during the civil war:

It was almost always winter in civil-war Petrograd. Spring and summer failed to bring the city to life. Instead, they brought the fear of cholera, the dust and dirt, the desire to leave to search for food …With shops and markets shut, street pedlars gone, factories silent, cab-drivers' livings gone with their dead horses, cafes, restaurants and clubs closed, and the printing presses silent, the bustling busy life of the central city simply faded away (264).

Arriving in St Petersburg in 1920, Bertrand Russell, a communist with high hopes for the new regime, summed up his conflicted responses to the city: "I am here at last, in this city which has filled the world with history, which has inspired the most deadly hatreds and the most poignant hopes." He referred to "a world of dying beauty and harsh life" and to "the destruction and cruelty upon which the ancient splendour was built" (Ayrton 190–92).

From what we know, it appears that my mother and her family were to some extent able to live a normal life during the Revolution, but life was always unpredictable. My mother said that she had been witness to a very violent event.

I don't know if I remember, or my mother told me, that the Bolsheviks came. They were looking for my father, who was in hiding. I must have been 3 or 4 [1918], something like that. He did live with us, but when the Revolution was on the way, he had to hide, and they asked my mother where he was, and she said she didn't know.

They weren't interested in her?

No, that was a different time. We had two burglaries. Once it was just things, the second time they were Bolsheviks, from the government, I suppose, and they wanted my father,

Why?

Well, because he was wealthy, he was bourgeois, that's all. And he had been in the army. I don't know. And they pointed a gun at my mother. She told me, I'm not sure ... no, I don't think I would have remembered. But I was there in a cot, and the man who was with him, he said, "Tell us or we'll shoot." And she said, "Shoot, then," and the other one said, "No, don't," and pointed to me, and I was in the cot, and they left, but of course afterwards they did find my father, and he was imprisoned.

This event seems to have taken place before the birth of my mother's brother, Mischa, in 1918. So was Dora pregnant at that time? When did Dmitri first get to see his son?

Many Jews, including the writer Isaac Babel, were sympathetic to the Revolution, hoping for the overthrow of a regime that they found restrictive, and feeling that being part of such a movement would lead to greater integration. It would appear that Dmitri was not one of them, though there is nothing to suggest that he was politically involved. It did not help that he was a former officer of the Imperial Army. Although some became officers in the new Red Army, which needed military experts, and some left Russia, others, like Dmitri, were considered "enemies", hunted down and arrested or shot. It turned out that in captivity Dmitri was told three times that he was to be shot. On three occasions — the first two supposedly as "a joke", the third for real, but with a last-minute reprieve. Was he then freed or did he escape? We will never know, but he did turn up in Riga some years later.

The city proved to be fertile ground for revolution; those in professional and artistic circles were trapped, squeezed between the extremes of aristocracy and industrial workers. At the outset, it was made clear that the Bolshevik government had no time for culture. When Lenin returned to Russia in 1905, he laid down the party line, which alienated many who had previously been sympathetic: "Nowadays we don't need theatre. Nor do we need music. We don't need articles about art or culture of any sort" (Ayrton, 144).

This from a land with such a rich heritage in every field of the arts from Pushkin and Chekhov to Glinka and Tchaikovsky, and a lively contemporary art scene that included the influential Russian avant-garde movement, with such names as Chagall and Kandinsky, Diaghilev and the filmmaker, Eisenstein, composers Scriabin, Prokofiev and Shostakovich.

However, once in power, the Bolsheviks changed their tune, finding that art could be a useful tool for government propaganda. The artistic communities were split: some fearing the power of the new regime; others seeing it as a sign of hope, leading to greater equality. They were quickly disenchanted. Some, like the writer Shmelev, welcomed the February Revolution and the fall of the autocracy, but rejected the October Revolution.

Bertrand Russell was in principle a supporter of the new regime, but, while acknowledging that he might have felt differently had he suffered, as many Russians had, from hunger and want, as he arrived in the country in 1920 he found that he did not react well to what he found in the country. He confessed himself "stifled by its utilitarianism, its indifference to love and beauty and the life of impulse" (Ayrton, 192).

In all ages, and throughout the world, the artistic community has often been at odds with the State. More in tune with deeper and more universal truths than political pragmatism, artists of all media are often by their very nature anti-establishment, and those who travel have access to reports beyond their own country's propaganda. So, as the Bolshevik government increased its grip, artists became fiercely resistant to its political manipulation, leading, in 1922, to a mass expulsion of artists and intellectuals.

Sometimes even the need to earn a living is overwhelmed by the need to speak out against despotic and divisive governments. Such rebellion is evident even as I write, with Russian writers, ballet dancers, and musicians risking their livelihood and liberty by speaking out against the invasion of Ukraine. Some of them, like dancer Olga Smirnova, are unable to stomach their country's activities, and, like a former generation, have defected to the West. In April 2023, the award-winning Russian novelist, Mikhail Shishkin, now living in exile, talked in an interview with the *Guardian* about the power of culture. He says that once the war is over, there will be a need to build bridges, and that "these bridges can be built only by culture, only by civilisation, only by literature and music. That will be the huge mission."

Shishkin's comments give a hint of the mysterious power that Russia has over its people, even those who have left. Something that touches on that elusive notion of a Russian "soul", a mysterious yet deep-rooted sense of identity that despite the furore of its history elicits love and loyalty in some who come to the country and are caught by its allure, and nostalgia in those who, like the composer Rachmaninov, were driven out or felt impelled to leave.

From the spring of 1917 to August 1920, the population of St Petersburg plummeted from two and a half million to three-quarters of a million, as members of the professional classes and aristocracy fled, and the military was mobilised. Those who left ranged from soldiers, officers, and Cossacks to intellectuals of various professions, dispossessed businessmen and landowners, as well as some anti-Bolshevik officials of the Russian Imperial government.

The outbreaks of cholera and typhus in 1918 also took their toll. During these years it was a city struggling for survival. As was Dora, alone with two small children. My mother told me:

"Oh yes, we were starving. But my mother sold some jewellery for meat and vegetables. No, we had no income. You couldn't buy food anyway, except if you paid an exorbitant amount or gave jewellery."

If you were lucky enough to have it.

The upheaval caused by the Revolution was to be felt for many years. Thousands of people fled the country. Those who remained lived with uncertainty and in difficult conditions. An English doctor, writing to his family in 1922, says:

Russia, between ourselves, is indescribable. Utter poverty, dirt, disease everywhere — everything degenerate, out of order and miserable. I have never imagined a country like it ... The people are charming — simple child-like peasants, and the steppe and forests are lovely but all else is misery and dirt personified. Lack of transport, lack of food, lack of every possible thing — not only in the Buzuluk area, but all over. Everyone practically is dressed in sacks or filthy sheepskins, and no one dares be neat and tidy, or they are accused of being bourgeois. (Melville Mackenzie, quoted by Sergei Nikitin)

This was written about the countryside. Although food was hard to come by, Moscow and St Petersburg escaped the worst of the famine of 1921–23, protected by a new law of food apportionment, in which grain was forcibly taken from the peasants, leading to thousands in the countryside dying of starvation.

Nonetheless, even in the cities, life was hard. It was only in 1922, after years of war and revolution, that the city began to recover. Poet Nina Berberova, returning to her beloved St Petersburg the previous year, saw a city with broken windows, boarded-up doors, and crumbling houses, with neighbours coming at night to take away doors and flooring. No cabs, few trams. But shops were just beginning to re-open and food reappear.

Escape

In 1920 Dora fled from St Petersburg, taking her children with her: Genia was five, Mischa 2. They headed for Dora's birthplace, Riga, where her parents still lived. My mother told me:

In the end we left. And I remember how we left, in a cattle truck, on hay, and it took a week to get from St Petersburg to Riga. Normally it wouldn't have taken so long. No, we weren't hiding in the hay. We were allowed to go because my mother's doctor gave her a certificate that she had TB, and that's how they let us go. One wasn't allowed to leave. That was 1920.

Like many refugees, the family was lucky to escape. Although the Treaty of Riga granting Latvian independence was signed in 1920, it did not come into effect until late in the year, and maybe its provisions did not filter down to the practice on the ground. In any case, in leaving her home and everything she owned, Dora must have been desperate. But the situation in St Petersburg was increasingly dangerous, Dmitri had left, and it was natural for her to head for a familiar and safe country, where she had lived before her marriage, and where she hoped to find her parents. It is hard to imagine how gruelling that journey must have been for a young woman with two small children, leaving behind everything she had known. Did she have TB, I wonder, or was a kindly doctor granting her the possibility of escape? In any case, at least there were some conditions for which leaving was possible. Unlike the Russian authorities twenty years later, for whom there could be no exceptions.

We don't know to what extent the family's fear was of the Bolsheviks, and how much their need to escape stemmed from a rising tide of antisemitism. Probably both. My mother has always referred to Russia as an antisemitic country, but we know nothing of how that was experienced in their St Petersburg life. Apart from my mother's grandfather, Bernhard, the family did not go to synagogue. We know nothing of their friends or social life; as an affluent professional family, they appear to have assimilated into the social and cultural life of the city.

At first, the Revolution seemed to bode well for the Jewish population.

The year 1917 transformed Jewish life, setting in motion a sudden and intense period of emancipation. Just days after the abdication of Tsar Nicholas II and the formation of the Provisional Government, all legal restrictions on Russian Jewry were lifted. More than 140 anti-Jewish statutes, totalling some 1,000 pages, were removed overnight. To mark this historic moment of abolition, a special meeting was convened by the Petrograd Soviet. Symbolically, the meeting happened to fall on 24 March 1917 — the eve of Passover (on-line summary of McGeever).

However, antisemitism did not disappear; in fact, shortage of food and accusations of hoarding led to rising hostility and increasing attacks on Jews, with a dramatic escalation in following years. Although pogroms had not been a feature of life in St Petersburg, by 1919 there was a fear that they might come, even there.

* * *

St Petersburg 2002

It was in much less troubled times that I arrived in St Petersburg in March 2002, near the end of a year's journey around the world. I had wanted to take my mother back to her birthplace for her eightieth birthday, but, saying how desperately she and her family had wanted to leave, she refused to go back.

My mother was often in my mind on the journey, especially as we approached Russia, then travelled across it. On one occasion, I stopped the car to take a photo of silver birch trees for her — the image that so often haunts Russian exiles. But it was on the trans-Siberian express that the countryside unfolded in all its glory. I wrote in my journal:

> I gazed out enchanted at the landscape of snow, firs, birches and little wooden houses each with their plots of ground with greenhouses with glass removed for the winter How could anyone say this journey was boring? Little dells, glades, valleys, utterly charming.

It was the landscape of my mother's childhood, of which she was still reminded by some precious Russian landscape paintings on her walls at home.

On my arrival, I phoned her, as I had from every country we visited.

"Where are you?" she asked.

"I'm in St Petersburg."

Intake of breath. "Oh ... and is it lovely?"

Despite her expressed dislike of Russia, and the difficulties of her early life there, in that moment I could hear that there was still a deep fondness for the city of her birth.

"Yes, Mum, it is lovely."

My journal continued:

> Well, everyone said it was lovely, and so it is: grand and gracious and beautifully proportioned. The long eighteenth-century buildings along the river Neva like a Canaletto painted in pastels. The Winter Palace in particular a glory in pale green and gold; the ethnological museum turquoise and white with a look of a wooden building: the first museum in the city. Everywhere graceful spires and domes.
>
> And the graciousness of the people!

The river Neva itself, flowing fast through the centre of the city, was thickened by little ice floes speeding downstream, reminders of a fierce winter just past. And, after travelling through Asia and the Americas, I experienced Europe as if for the first time, and realised how much we take for granted. The richness of the culture, and this: a city steeped in history.

We stayed just a block from the Mariinsky Theatre, home to the Kirov, and were able simply to walk around to book for the ballet. Here, at last, was the city culture my then partner Stephen had craved; a city to walk in, to breathe in, and to feel the balance of its eighteenth-century buildings and streets; the beauty of its baroque churches. I was revelling in *War and Peace*, so many of its scenes set in these buildings, when czars held sway and the grand houses opened their doors to the gentry for parties and evenings of cards.

And the ballet! I'd always associated the romance of ballet with Russia — Tchaikovsky, and all those graceful swans! All those famous dancers too, including some, like Nureyev, who came to the UK. For me, Russia was the home of ballet. To our delight we were able to get tickets for "Romeo and Juliet" one evening — only the most expensive seats were available, but the outlay was worthwhile. A touching portrayal, magnificent dancing, and an orchestra of authentic Russian authority.

We do not know how Dora and her family spent their time. Did they too go to the ballet? It seems likely. By the nineteenth century, Russian ballet had become renowned throughout the world, and a symbol of high culture for educated Russians. There is little documentation about pre-Revolutionary middle-class cultural life: history has concentrated on the grand aristocracy and the life of the poor, on the deep inequality and centuries of oppression that gave rise to revolution. Being half-Russian, I have always felt touched by that struggle that has continued, in various guises, over the centuries. Under the Czar or Bolsheviks, Stalin, perestroika or Putin, the lot of the Russian people seems to be that of endurance.

As a long-term foreign Russian resident commented in 2023:

Dissent was always a serious matter here. I never understood the logic and purposefulness of the responses. And again it just carries on down this road to nowhere. (And people die in large numbers).

Riga, 1920–22

Riga, in Latvia, was my grandmother's birthplace. As can be seen from the 1911 atlas inherited from my mother, Latvia, like Ukraine, was at that time part of the Russian Empire; Dora's nationality was Russian. We don't know when she moved to St Petersburg, but presumably on or just before her marriage in 1914. Her parents continued to live there, so when Dora and the children fled from St Petersburg, Riga was a natural place of refuge. It was a cultured city, with a long history of Jewish settlement.

In the nineteenth century, Riga was a Western-facing city. With a community of immigrants with no fixed religious or cultural traditions, Riga was open to cultural diversity, and its buoyant economy made it an attractive destination for Jews from Russia and other parts of Eastern Europe. Economic prosperity continued until the end of the 1920s. The Jewish population, which was largely upper middle class, established and ran many kinds of businesses and factories, as well as importing and exporting a variety of raw materials. They also worked in banking and other financial institutions, as well as in professions such as medicine and law.

At the beginning of the twentieth century, the number of Jews in Riga grew rapidly, reaching more than 30,000 before the First World War. During that war, approximately one-third of the Jews left, though many later returned. In 1918 the Republic of Latvia was established as a liberal democracy, granting general suffrage and equal rights to all citizens, and cultural autonomy to minorities, and after initial difficulties, by 1920 Latvia had signed an agreement with Soviet Russia and Germany to confirm its independence. Andrew Ezergailis writes: "During Latvia's years as an independent republic … there were no anti-Jewish laws. From 1934 to 1940 anti-Semitism was banned" (79).

From 1918 to 1940, Riga was the capital of this independent Latvia, and under the Latvian regime, the community included some 40,000 Jews, more than ten per cent of the population. The community had a well-developed network of Hebrew and Yiddish schools, as well as a lively Jewish cultural life. Jews were integrated into most aspects of life in Riga and even sat on the city council. Until the Germans came, there had never been a pogrom in Latvia. It had even become known as "the Jewish country".

When Dora and her children arrived in Riga in 1920, my mother relates:

> We went to the flat of my mother's parents. She didn't know if they were alive or dead, and she didn't know if my father was alive or dead. And she rang the bell and we went up the steps, and there was no reply. And she had no money, nowhere to go. So we sat on the steps, and Mischa and I were playing with a ball, and then an old man came up the stairs with a stick and a hat and a white collar, as they were dressed then, and then they spoke. He was crying. He thought we were dead. They had had no contact for years, they couldn't.

It was her grandfather.

It is striking how often the words "couldn't", and "weren't allowed to" appear in my mother's account of the early part of her life. For those of us used to freedom of movement and communication both within and between countries, it is hard to imagine such frequent constraints.

They stayed for only two years in Latvia. Genia went to school there, but it was not a country that she liked, unlike their next port of call, the country in which they stayed for more than ten years, and where they settled at last: Switzerland.

Switzerland, 1922–35

Several members of our family found themselves in Switzerland after fleeing from St Petersburg, though they were scattered, with some in the French-speaking part near Geneva, and some, like Dora and her children, in the German part.

My mother was seven when she and Dora arrived in the ancient town of Chur, in the mountainous region of Grisons, on the banks of the Rhine. It was where her aunt Becca lived with her husband Franz, a Swiss examining magistrate. After the uncertainties of life in Russia and Riga, Genia found it a haven. Sadly, in the interview, we did not get as far as Switzerland, but over the years she had always spoken with great warmth about her time there. She loved the Swiss, whom she found always kind, and the country and their life there also fed her romantic tendencies. For they lived in a castle. Owned by friends of the family, Haldenstein Castle had been built in the sixteenth century, in the German-speaking Canton of Graubünden. It's a strikingly handsome building, set at the foot of the Calanda mountain, with extensive views, and now offering guided tours as a Swiss heritage site of national significance. My mother took great pride at having lived in such a historic place, and had a picture of it on a wall of her London sitting room.

Genia attended a local school; when he was older, her brother went to a grammar school, their schooling paid for by the generosity of Uncle Sasha, still in Riga. As a child, my mother recalls being dressed in a white coat, almost invisible against the snow, and being teased by local boys, who stuffed snow down her neck. But she was happy playing with her brother and her cousin Lilik, the son of her cousin Berthe, who seemed to be frequent visitors. The three of them formed quite a band, and remained close for the rest of their lives.

When Genia was little, a local couple, who had no children of their own, offered to take her for walks, but Dora wasn't keen, and my mother went only once and was bored. She made friends with a number of girls at school, and stayed in touch with some of them well into old age. She also got to know a local bookshop owner, who seems to have been quite an influence. We don't know how much Dora was with her family in Switzerland, only that she spent a lot of time in Riga, to care for her elderly mother.

In her teens, Genia took great pleasure in skiing and hiking, often alone, in her beloved mountains. And she was discovering literature, a love that stayed with her for the rest of her life. There were also less pleasurable memories. Kept to one wing of a building that belonged to others, my mother felt constrained and was sure that it was haunted. The owner kept an Alsatian, which went mad and bit its owner, and also attacked my mother, pinning her to the ground. She wasn't hurt, but traumatised, and the incident set her against Alsatians for the rest of her life. She also felt bullied by Becca and said that that led to her agreeing to an early marriage to get away.

After her schooldays, my mother was sent, very much against her will, to a commercial college run by Catholic nuns. She was able to finish the much-hated three-year course in two years, and got a diploma in German shorthand and typing. In 1933 she was allowed to go to Paris, where she obtained a diploma in the teaching of French at the Faculté des Lettres at the Sorbonne. Being in Paris was a joy, a taste of freedom in a life where she had been able to make few choices of her own.

After one year at the Sorbonne, she had to leave: there was only enough money to pay for one university education and her brother Mischa, as a man, took precedence. Genia did get her diploma, but always harboured an exaggerated respect for academic success, not least that of Mischa, who made the most of his opportunity, worked his way through part of his time at university, and went on to have a distinguished academic career.

In Switzerland, as in many other European countries, attitudes toward the Jews have fluctuated. Their right to settle freely was not restored with the Swiss constitution of 1848, and was only granted after approval in a referendum. The right was strengthened with the revised constitution of 1874, guaranteeing the freedom of religion. In 1876, the Jews were granted full equality in civil rights and were allowed to travel. In 1920, the Jewish population reached its peak at 21,000 people (0.5% of the total population), a figure that has remained almost constant ever since.

During the First and Second World Wars Switzerland maintained a stance of armed neutrality, and apart from minor skirmishes was not involved militarily. Living there, however, was not without its insecurities, since the fall of France to the Germans in June 1940 meant that for most of the war Switzerland was completely surrounded by Germany and its allies.

Because of its neutral status, Switzerland was considered a safe haven for refugees. Most of its citizens supported the Allies, and many, including Genia's in-laws, helped support those who had fled the Nazi threat. But its neutrality did not stretch to protection of the Jews. Had she stayed in her beloved adopted land, Genia might have had a less rosy view of the Swiss. In the Second World War the Swiss government persuaded Germany to stamp "J" on the passport of Jews in order to make it easier to refuse them admission. And those who were admitted received a lower level of financial support. In 2002, the Bergier Commission concluded that, in common with other countries, Switzerland had not only refused many thousands of Jews entry into Switzerland, but had also handed over some to the Germans. The report also confirmed the allegation that assets in the amount of several million of francs were declared dormant.

And the shadows were to fall even on my mother's cherished home in Chur. In 2023 it was revealed that a large obelisk in Chur cemetery, in the city centre, was in fact placed there by the Germans on the eve of the Second World War, a monument to Nazi propaganda. A testimony to the presence in the 1930s of many Nazi organisations in the town, it was a blight, too, on the prized neutrality of the Swiss. At the time, says Swiss historian Martin Bucher, Chur's residents must have known what it was. "On Nazi holidays they put Swastikas on this monument ... people would have seen it was a Nazi monument." (https://www.bbc.co.uk/news/world-europe-65099516)

But my mother had gone by then and knew nothing of this. She loved Switzerland: she always talked fondly of the Swiss and her time there, and later in life returned there for holidays.

* * *

In 2023, I was coming to the end of writing this book, when I went to Geneva to stay with Mischa's widow, Poury. Despite the fact that she had claimed in our exchange of emails that she had nothing to contribute, and that Mischa had never spoken of his parents, I was sure that when we met, as we talked, more would emerge. And so it proved.

What I learned led me to question my former understanding of events. Apparently, the reason Dora chose to go to Switzerland was two-fold: the fact that Becca and her husband were already living there, and the need of Mischa, who was asthmatic, to gain from the benefit of the mountain air. I had always assumed — been led to believe — that both children accompanied their mother from St Petersburg to Riga and then on to Switzerland. Poury, however, claimed that Mischa had been alone with Becca and Franz in Chur. She was under the impression that this had been a permanent separation from his mother; she didn't know that Dora and Genia were there too, that they had also lived in Haldenstein. I knew from the many details of what my mother told me that she and Dora had been there. But Poury was adamant that Mischa had been sent to Switzerland when he was two, which would have been in 1920, the year they left St Petersburg and went to Riga.

Did Mischa not go to Riga, but straight to Switzerland? But there is that vivid picture of my mother and him playing with a ball on the steps of their grandparents' house. I can only think that he stayed in Riga for a while, then was sent to stay with Becca in Switzerland with Dora and Genia coming two years later. Two years without his mother at the age of two. It was only in piecing together what my mother had told me and what Mischa had told Poury that we found a way of reconciling the two accounts. In all of this we were reliant not just on memories, but on conflicting memories of memories. And then, just as we seemed to have arrived at the truth, came further information: the astounding evidence from Dora's passport that she had been a resident, voting, in Riga during the late 1920s. It seems that at some point Dora did leave her children with their aunt; that Poury's version, after all, was nearer "the truth".

It's been hard to assimilate such a different version of what I have understood all my life. Hard to reconcile the rosy picture of a largely happy childhood with the reality of a beloved mother who was missing for much of the time. With this news, my mother's account of her aunt's bullying acquires a new force.

Mischa also loved Switzerland. He was educated there and worked there for most of his life. It was his country, and he considered himself to be Swiss. When offered a high-profile job in the States, he refused, feeling that the country that had educated him deserved his loyalty. Much later in life, when living in Geneva, he revisited Haldenstein with Poury, his second wife. Although the building itself — by then a national heritage site — was closed that day, they went around the outside. Mischa pointed out the window of what had been his room, and showed Poury how the bars had been forced apart so that, as a child, or maybe a teenager, he could escape!

Egypt, 1935–45

In 1935, at the age of twenty, Genia married Felix, a German-born Swiss eighteen years her senior. Felix was a lecturer in Spanish and French at Alexandria University, so on their marriage, they moved to Egypt. He had returned to Switzerland presumably during a university holiday and, when he proposed to my mother, apparently gave her just one week to make up her mind.

One week! Obviously, after her disappointment at having to leave the Sorbonne, Genia was ready to embrace a new adventure, all the more so if her mother had left. So Genia moved with her new husband to Cairo, where she recaptured some of the freedom of her year in Paris, albeit now as a married woman. The sense of freedom did not last long, and Cairo was not altogether the haven that she might have imagined. In the period just before the Second World War, the whole region was in an uneasy state.

In 1939, my brother Eric was born, and two years later, after five years of marriage, Felix fell ill. He had had rheumatic fever in his youth, and his heart was always weak. He went to Palestine for medical treatment, but in August 1941 died suddenly from an embolism on the lung. It was only after my visit to Jerusalem in 1995 that my mother told me that it was in the Jewish cemetery there that Felix had been buried.

After his death, Genia and Eric stayed on in Cairo and, alone in wartime Egypt, in yet another country, with responsibility for a small child, and a need to earn her living, Genia had to call on all her reserves of resilience. First of all, she taught French in an Egyptian government school for girls, and then worked for the recently established British inter-Service Middle East Intelligence Centre (MEIC) GHQ at a monitoring centre, where she transcribed French and German broadcasts. Her knowledge of German shorthand, acquired during those detested secretarial studies in Switzerland, came in extremely useful. She was presumably gradually learning English at this time, though a number of her colleagues were German speakers — presumably Jews — so could translate for her when necessary. Later in life, she claimed to have been the first person to have received news of the German surrender at Stalingrad.

The British had a long history in Egypt. They first occupied it in 1882, during the Anglo-Egyptian War. Although Egypt was never part of the British Empire, it was for many years a formal protectorate. In 1936, the UK and Egyptian governments signed a treaty under which the UK was required to withdraw all military forces from Egypt, other than those required to protect the Suez Canal and its surrounding areas, and limiting the number of British troops allowed in Egypt to 10,000. The UK also agreed to train and equip the Egyptian Army. With the outbreak of the Second World War, although Egypt was neutral and remained nominally independent, the British retook effective control of the country, which became an important military base in the Middle East.

The British presence was not popular with most Egyptians; many saw it as oppressive, and openly supported the Germans.

Even though Egypt had broken relations with the Axis, she had not declared war; many Egyptians vented their pro-Nazi sympathies loudly; student demonstrators ran through the streets shouting slogans in favour of Rommel; secret agents of the Axis powers moved in the shadows, spying freely and spreading demoralisation. (Le Vernoy, 111)

In 1943, my mother met my English father, also called Eric, at a friend's house. At 24, he was three years younger than her and only a few years out of Oxford, He was working for MI8, the signals intelligence department of the War Office, in charge of a unit which intercepted German messages and sent them for decoding to Bletchley in Buckingham (the Enigma machine). He was awarded an MBE for distinguished services rendered; I still have the rather battered medal with a letter signed by George VI, expressing his disappointment at not being able to present it to my father in person.

I also came across my father's letter asking for permission to marry — a necessary procedure, since my mother was not a British citizen — which, after some bureaucratic correspondence, was duly granted on a very small piece of flimsy paper. "Sanction is given under GHQ MEF letter (reference) dated 26 Mar 43, for the marriage between Capt, E.G.G. HANROTT and Mrs E WEIL."

The marriage took place on 6th April 1943, and as a result, Genia acquired British citizenship.

During the war, Cairo was full of British soldiers. Generally, troops were stationed in camps around the city, while officers lived in the city itself. The couple and baby Eric took a flat with a large terrace in the smart residential area of Zamalek, and were often host to men coming in from the desert. Many of my father's Oxford friends were in Cairo during the war, some of them stationed in the desert. My parents were able to put some of them up, and, as my mother said, "make them feel at home". My brother Eric, who, remarkably, has many memories of that time, says there was a lot of coming and going, and many men in uniforms. He remembers that everywhere on the pavement near their flat were squashed cockroaches. When he came to England, he couldn't understand why there were no cockroaches!

My brother (known as "little Eric", though he grew to be much taller than his father!), says that war was omnipresent. He was not scared but Genia told him later that she had been very frightened in the days before the battle of Alam Halfa, the turning point of the Desert War, just before El Alamein, when

Rommel's Afrika Korps had advanced to the Egyptian frontier, just a day's travel from Cairo. The night before the battle, she heard lorries thundering through the streets all night, and was told that the Germans would invade the following day. As a Jewish woman, and one working for the British, she was terrified.

> [With] the 8th Army in retreat, it seemed as though nothing could halt the Axis advance. Those Egyptians who saw the Germans as potential liberators from British repression were already preparing to welcome the invaders (Hodgkin, 274).

Expectations of a German invasion led to the British evacuating a number of departments of Middle East headquarters from Cairo. The railway station was besieged with people anxious to flee before the Germans arrived. Like others, my mother sought and got permission from the Egyptian Ministry of the Interior to send little Eric to Palestine for his safety, initially from September 1942 to January 1943, then extended until the following September. He was only three. Although for different reasons, Eric, like his uncle Mischa, was sent away by his mother at a very young age. A strange echo of the past.

We don't know why my mother did not go with him. It could be that she fell foul of the quota that the British, in an effort to keep a balance between the Arab and Jewish communities, had imposed on Palestine; it could have been that she felt unable to leave her job — she did need to keep earning a living, and her work was increasingly important. Or, as my brother said rather cynically, it could be that she wanted to continue living it up in Cairo.

For some reason, my brother said, the Egyptians made difficulties about his return, so his new father (also Eric) arranged for him to come back to Egypt in a British army lorry.

My brother still remembers the trip with pleasure, and thinks that one of my father's friends from Oxford was in command of that convoy. What an adventure for a four-year-old boy! But it must have been hard for my mother to let him go. In a letter from Switzerland dated August 1943, her first husband's sister Hilde asks if my mother had been able to visit him, or at least get regular news from those she describes as those "*gentilles personnes*" (kind people) in Palestine.

Eric remembers that Mr and Mrs Ucko were indeed kind. They were German Jews who had made a home in what was then Palestine, and he was very comfortable on their little farm near Ramataim, far from the tensions between Arabs and Jews which would lead to the upheavals caused by the setting up of the State of Israel in 1948. The couple even wanted to adopt him. He doesn't remember Genia visiting him, but said that my father, the other Eric whom my mother had recently married, did. The people he was staying with said, "Here's your father", whereupon Eric, aged three, said, "This isn't my father." Apparently, they had never met. What an extraordinary first meeting! And how my brother must have missed his mother. He remembers having a toy telephone on which he pretended to phone her.

Another time, another place, another war. In some ways, there are extraordinary parallels between St Petersburg in 1915–20 and the Cairo of the early 1940s. In each case, there was not only a world war, but each was suffering from internal political ferment. In the Russia of my mother's childhood, the Revolution; in the Egypt of her adulthood, the seething turmoil of Middle Eastern politics under an unpopular British occupation.

In wartime Cairo and Alexandria, rather like St Petersburg during the First World War and Revolution, some normal life continued; there was still an active cultural and society life and, unlike rationed wartime England, an abundance of delicacies for those fortunate enough to be able to afford them. The British established working hours of 9–1 and 4 or 5 till 8 or 9, with a clear division between officers and other ranks. Officers often frequented the fashionable Gezira club, which at the time was for the exclusive use of the British Army, with tennis and swimming, dinner and dancing.

And, just as upper-class cultural and social life continued in St Petersburg as many people ignored the existence of war, so it was in wartime Cairo. The blackout was barely observed. My mother's French cousin, Lilik, arriving in Cairo to fight with the British, saw how

> long lines of ambulances carrying wounded from the front traversed the city; men in bandages and plaster casts leaned on their canes as they strolled along the streets; revellers on leave still had the drawn faces and haunted look of battle in their eyes.
>
> However, the city itself seemed indifferent to the war raging in the deserts of Tripolitania and Cyrenaica; Cairo was an oasis of bygone luxuries: hot baths; cool beer at the golf club, the Cricket Club or the Gezira Tennis Club; opulent nightclubs featuring belly-dancers; and last, but not least, Madame Badia's girls. (Le Vernoy, 111)

Vivien Leigh, visiting Egypt during the Second World War, is quoted as saying: "The war is non-existent in Egypt and to see large tables spread with all sorts of deliciousnesses and bowls of cream was extraordinary" (Cooper, 250). She was of course referring to the ex-pat community. Eric's memory, as we have heard, is of a very different experience. For a couple working, respectively, in the army and for the British government, his parents' lives were much more involved in the war, even if they did enjoy some of the pleasures of Cairo's glittering social life. When my father was promoted to Major, my parents apparently held a big party on the large terrace of their flat; like many other officers, they also frequented the Gezira club, where Eric remembers going for a swim. As a small child, he was petrified!

Other ranks, of course, were barred from such places. To keep up the morale of British troops during this time, newscasts from Britain were broadcast from local and British transmitters, throughout the Middle East. As the magazine, *Parade*, itself specifically for this readership, explains in its issue of 17 May 1941,

> Burnt and battered a bit — but by no means shattered — by Fritz and his *blitz*, London yet calls the world right through the day and night for a total of twenty-one hours out of the twenty-four. And calls the world not in English only. To millions of British subjects London speaks in their own tongues. To foreign countries it broadcasts daily, in 32 languages, a matter of 59 News Bulletins ... London is still the great fountain-head to which people of Europe and elsewhere turn for news ... And none more eagerly or more trustfully than those in the enemy and enemy-occupied countries, who listen at the risk of liberty or life.
>
> And what about us? you may ask — the soldiers, sailors and airmen from all parts of the Empire who are serving overseas?

Parade paints a rosy picture in its coverage, whether of Palestine, the Western Desert or, indeed, London. With pictures of Sandy Macpherson and the BBC theatre organ and a group of singers, it lists some of the BBC highlights of the time:

A feature of the farmer's role in the war
    Hear farmers and farmhands from the West Country, Norfolk and the West Riding of Yorkshire speaking from their homes, fields and pubs
    "Front Line Family" episode 19

The adventures of the British Family Robison in wartime London
Gold dust for the homesick soldier.

As the heading in the issue "Hello Middle East! London Calling!" implies, this was particularly important for the troops in the Western Desert.

The nightly pilgrimage over the desert to the nearest radio, probably perched among the Stella bottles in the Naafi dugout, is an off-duty phenomenon peculiar to this war. Through the radio the present-day soldier in the field is more closely linked with his homeland and the outer world than his opposite number in any other war.

Such importance is attached to entertaining the troops through the radio that separate programmes specially for the men in the Middle East are broadcast.

And week by week it gave crucial information of the British view of how the war was progressing. In the issue of 25 July 1942, under the title "Desert Pendulum", it describes the local situation:

The battle in the Western Desert which has for so many months resembled the ebb and flow of a tide, with the fighting surging from east to west, west to east, has during the last week swung like a pendulum from south to north and back again. The battle centre has shifted nearly every day from Himeimat near the Qatara Depression to Tel el Eisa on the coastal sector, then to Ruweisat Ridge, the five mile lozenge running east and west in the centre.

My mother was in a rather different position from other army wives. She had already been living in Cairo for a number of years with her first husband. Since she had taught at a government school and Felix had taught at the university, she was perhaps more in touch with local people. In all, Genia lived in Egypt for ten years, As was common for the European middle classes of the time, they had servants, including a Bedouin nurse for Eric, whom my mother accused of giving him fleas! Genia acquired some "kitchen" Arabic, discovering that it had an even richer vocabulary of swear words than German! She was always rather racist about Arabs. She didn't take to the Egyptians, except the poorer classes, whom she liked.

Most English-speaking people in the city at that time were under thirty. There were few European women, except prostitutes. Photos often show Genia surrounded by handsome young men and in dashing open-topped cars. She was young and very beautiful, so as a "merry widow" she had her share of suitors. Later, there were many photos of her, my father and their friends — some of whom remained close for the rest of their lives.

When they were not working, she and my father went riding. My mother took riding lessons from a Russian former cavalry officer. She spoke of the magnificent Arab horses, and always retained a love of horses. It seems to have been a happy time.

She acquired a love of the desert — a love I've inherited — and she talked of one episode when she went with my father for a meeting with a sheikh in his tent in the desert. As was the custom, she was ushered into the sheikh's harem, a tent full of large and cheerful women. As a sign of wealth, being fat was fashionable. One woman passed around a basket of sweets. Genia took one, whereupon the woman took a handful and put them in her lap.

In Egypt, as for my mother in Russia as a child, they left the heat of the city in the summer to escape to cooler climes, in this case to Alexandria. I think my mother took such a way of life for granted, not really taking on board that such escapes were not available to the poor in Russia nor to the ordinary British troops in Egypt. Although Alexandria was subject to bombing raids during the war, Artemis Cooper says that Laurence Durrell's Alexandria Quartet portrays it as "a city bathed in glamorous corruption" (253).

* * *

I have visited Cairo twice, once in 2000, and about ten years earlier. On neither visit did I think much about my parents' experiences — it was such a different country then. My first visit was to go to Luxor and the Valley of the Kings, the second, as a jumping off point for the desert. What a different city Cairo had become — or reverted to in peacetime, as an independent country, free from strategic and colonial influence. A noisy, crowded vibrant city: full of markets, cafes with wonderful food, roadside vendors, including people able to mend any kind of appliance.

I found the people very friendly but remember only one interaction. I was on a train, trying to get off, but almost forcibly prevented by a vast crowd of people getting on. I had to fight my way off, and found myself on the platform shaking, in tears. A young man came up to me, proffering a handkerchief, and saying, "I apologise for my country."

Riga, 1941: Dora

Passport to freedom

We don't know how much time Dora spent with her parents in Riga. My understanding was that while she and her children were living in Switzerland, she made frequent trips to Riga. However, in 2023 a Latvian friend deciphering her passport discovered that there were records of annual registrations in Riga throughout the late 1920s, and of her voting in 1928, though for some reason in 1930, Dora's passport was changed to a foreign one. It's also possible that when Genia and Mischa were grown up and married, Dora went to live there permanently. As we've seen, Riga was a peaceful tolerant place to live — until 1941, when first the Soviets, then the Nazis, moved in.

When my mother was married and living in Cairo, she, and later baby Eric, made several visits to Riga to see her mother and grandparents. Married to a Swiss citizen, with a Swiss passport, Genia was able to come and go. The last of those visits — and the last time she saw her family — was in 1940. At the end of their visit, my mother and Eric travelled back from Riga to Egypt by train via Italy, where they apparently stayed with one of Genia's school friends. It was a long journey, particularly slow at this time of wartime disruption, and, crucially, one that entailed crossing Nazi Germany. One can only imagine the ordeal for a Jewish woman travelling in carriages full of German soldiers, at every moment fearing that she would be challenged. We still have that historic passport with its many stamps, which date the journey, including a Nazi one of a swastika held in the claws of an eagle. Eric, no doubt tuning into his mother's fear, apparently howled throughout the journey.

The rest of the family were not so lucky. The following year, the Nazis took over the city, and with some 24,000 others, Dora, Sasha and their mother were killed. Paulina was 86; Dora,57;

Sasha a couple of years older. Though it was some years before my mother heard of their fate, she never got over the fact that she left her mother there.

Mischa from Switzerland and my mother from Egypt tried everything they could to trace Dora, to get her a visa, and to get her out of Riga. One of the most moving things I found when going through my mother's papers was a carbon copy of the letter, typed on a manual typewriter, an application that she had sent to the URSS legation consular service on 7 November 1944, referring to a visit she had made to the legation the previous day:

Details de ma mère, Dora Fischberg
   Nom: FISCHBERG, DORA, née Arenson
   Nationalité: Russe
   Date et lieu de naissance: née en 1995 [misprint: actually 1884] à Riga
   Dernière addresse: 26 Daugavas iels [iela], Riga.
   Apparentée à famille Berman, Tukkum

[Apparantée (connected by marriage to) the Berman family; Tukums, a small town in Latvia, near where her parents lived for a while.]

It was to no avail. Dora was in fact already dead, but it was not until after the war that my mother, by then in England, learned of Dora's fate. My brother, then about seven years old, remembers her receiving a letter from a neighbour which broke the news of Dora's death some six years before, and my mother's inconsolable crying.

The last address given in that application is a telling one. It was right in the middle of the ghetto to which Jews had been forced to move in October 1941. The ghetto was surrounded by a double barbed wire fence; residents were "forced to live in confined and brutal circumstances; their mobility and ability to get real news was circumscribed ... they were living under terror and duress" (Ezergailis, 16).

They were forbidden to leave; cut off from the world. In her compelling and often harrowing account, Frida Michelson, one of the few survivors of that time, paints a starkly graphic picture of life and conditions in the ghetto. 30,000 people were squeezed into a compound of a few streets, with only four square metres of space per person allowed. The buildings were infested with fleas, mice and cockroaches, with few functioning facilities. Only one shop was permitted for the inhabitants, with meagre provisions which had to be supplemented by a few non-Jews willing to sell goods at exorbitant prices. Michelson describes how the inhabitants, forced from their own homes, tried to create some kind of family life, even create some semblance of normality: to sanitise, scrub everything; at night stashing any little valuables left to them into the cracks of the crumbling walls. In the compound, they were cold, hungry and humiliated; terrified of what might come.

By the time my mother wrote that letter to the Soviet authorities, the ghetto had been liquidated and the inhabitants were dead. It was closed in November 1943.

As I was researching this book, it was well-nigh intolerable to come across an account by a woman who worked for the Nazis under occupation and in 1944 was evacuated by the Germans to Riga, where her family lived in an apartment in that very former Jewish ghetto, whose inhabitants had been killed or sent to camps. She blithely recalled that "the apartment was sparse, but still furnished." Unimaginable.

In August 1940, the Soviet Union annexed Latvia, and Riga became the capital of the Latvian Soviet Socialist Republic. Antisemitic Nazi propaganda exploded in 1941, linking Jews to communism. In what Ezergailis calls "the propaganda of the streets", Jews lost their citizenship, synagogues were burned

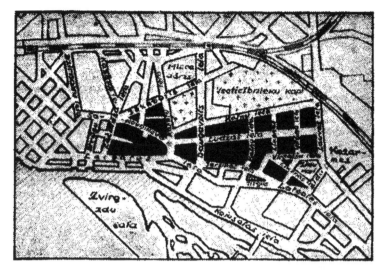

Ar melnu apzīmēti kvartāli, kuros paredz nometināt visus Rīgas žīdus.

The caption reads "the area marked in black represents the area that the Jews will be moved to and held".

and property was first looted and then expropriated. German forces occupied Riga in early July 1941, and immediately afterwards the elimination of the Jewish and Roma population began. 30,000 Jews were shot in the autumn of 1941, with most of the remaining Jewish people being rounded up and put into ghettos. In November and December 1941 the Riga Ghetto became crowded and to make room for the imminent arrival of German Jews, who were being shipped into the country, all the remaining Jews in Riga were taken from the ghetto to the nearby Rumbula Forest and shot.

We don't know how long Dora had been in Riga: maybe just long enough to be caught; maybe longer. It seems likely that she and her family were subject to the humiliation, the degradation of the months before the deaths: the forced labour, being forced to wear the Star of David, to walk not on the pavements but in the gutter. Sasha and their parents were long-term residents; did their neighbours betray them?

My mother never forgave the Germans. Did Dora? History has extraordinary examples of forgiveness of torturers, of forgiveness even at the moment of death. How did she face her death? At first, I wondered if there had been any consolation at going together with her beloved mother and brother, then discovered from a survivor's account that families were split up — that the fit and young, those able to work, were sent to a different part of the ghetto from the children, the old and the frail; that for some younger Jews death was deferred by allocation to slave labour in the city or in the fields.

We can't know what Dora and her family felt. Terror, of course, and maybe that shut out everything else. Was there any flashback to that other gun pointed at her in her St Petersburg flat all those years before, that more compassionate gun, which was pointed away at the sight of the child in her cot? Unlike the flight from Russia, facilitated by a kindly doctor, from Riga there was to be no permission to leave. This time there was no escape.

Dora and Dmitri had each been threatened by guns in St Petersburg. This time, some twenty years later, faced by the guns not of their own countrymen but of Germans, there was no reprieve. Only by searching the Hall of Names did we discover that my grandfather Dmitrijs Zāmuels Fisberga was also a victim of the *Shoah*, the Holocaust. And that he was born in 1885 and lived in Latvia. His place of birth is given, and, with the help of an expert translator, we have at last been able to decipher it. It was only in 2023, more than a year after the Russian invasion of Ukraine, that I learned that my grandfather was born there. Dmitri's place of birth was Mohilev in Podolia Guberniya (a province in present-day Ukraine), now known as Mohyliv-Podilskyi. No details of the time, place or manner of his death are known.

So, in 1941:

Dora was killed

Felix died of a pulmonary embolism

Genia became a widow at the age of 26. She probably also became an orphan. She certainly lost her mother that year. As Dmitri was living in Latvia, it is highly likely that he too was killed in 1941.

Holocaust

For most of my life, I believed that my grandmother had died, gassed, in a concentration camp. Even as late as 2004, I wrote about that understanding. It was, and still is, the generally understood concept of what the Holocaust entailed. It is how the Holocaust is generally perceived. I think this first version was what my mother told me, though it was not something we ever talked about. There would be a mention of Dora, the topic would rise to the surface, my mother's grief would emerge, and we swiftly moved on to something else.

And then the story changed. It was only late in my mother's life that she told me — had she just discovered? — that Dora had died in Riga, and that she had been shot. That, along with her brother and their mother, Dora had had to dig her own grave, and then was shot. How would my mother have discovered this new truth? Maybe it came from my nephew's family research.

And my great-grandfather, that pious Jew, Bernhard? I've always understood that it was Dora, Sasha and their mother Paulina who died on that day. But my daughter said that my mother told her that there were four of them, including Bernhard: a different story from the one my mother had told me and my brother all our lives. Searching again in the Hall of Names at Yad Vashem, I found the name of a Bernhards Aronsons, born in 1844, living in Latvia — I thought it might well have been him. But, in the entry for Paulina, her status is listed as "widow". Did he die in an earlier phase of the atrocity or did he die before it all began? How and by how much Bernhard predeceased his wife we don't know.

The only evidence we have of the fate of our family is from the Hall of Names on the Yad Vashem site. It's an incredible resource, but with so many different spellings of the same names, it can be confusing. Fischberg also appears as Fisberg and Fischbergs, among others; and Dora's maiden name as Aronson, Aaronson, Aronsons, and so on. Only from the documents provided — the passports of Dora, Dmitri and Paulina, which were handed into the police — can we be sure of their identity, and in some cases of their fate; for some individuals it is noted that their fate is unknown.

In any case, it would seem that the second of my mother's versions of the death of her family was also inaccurate. Reading documentation of the carefully planned methods used for the killing of Jews in Riga, and survivor accounts, it appears that the reality was different. It would seem pretty clear that Dora was killed along with some 24,000 other Jews, on 30 November or 6 December 1941, taken from the Riga ghetto where they had been forced to live, and driven on foot in a column the ten or so kilometres to Rumbula, an uninhabited swampy marshy area chosen for its accessibility and suitably soft ground.

Victims were stripped of their valuables, made to put them in a box, then made to undress. They were then forced to lie down in a deep pit on top of each other, and were shot in the back of the neck.

There are different versions of who carried out the attacks. While it is clear that the whole atrocity was planned by the Germans, there is clear evidence of Latvian complicity, probably not in the killing itself — carried out, it would seem by a mere twelve men — but in shepherding the Jewish victims to the site. The Germans were part of what were known, not only in Latvia but across the region from the Baltic to the Black Sea, as Action Squads, SS men with the specific task of shooting Jews. Face-to-face killings in what has been called Holocaust by Bullets. Little has been written, and few seem to know, about the fact that

Jews were killed not only in the camps but in the places where they lived. That the main method of genocide in Eastern Europe was Holocaust by Bullets: the mass slaughter of some one and a half million Jews. It was in other areas that more "efficient", more "scientific" methods of killing took over.

Survivor accounts say that on November 30th the well-drilled and largely secret activity started at 4 am and ended at 5pm when it got dark. At the ghetto, some, reduced to a kind of docility by months of humiliation and starvation, and accepting death as preferable to continued suffering, simply gave up. Others did not go gentle into that dark night. As they were rounded up, survivor accounts tell of how some fought, and ran, trying to escape. Those resisting or those elderly and infirm who were unable to keep up were killed in the ghetto itself, leaving a trail of bloody clothes and bodies. At the killing ground, death was accompanied by prayer, screams, cries, the clutching of loved ones.

Extraordinarily, a few people managed to escape and play dead, and one woman, Frida Michelson, survived long enough to tell the harrowing story. After undressing with the others, she fell into the snow and pretended to be dead. As she lay there, barely daring to breathe, she felt a hail of heavy weights land on her — the shoes that the others had been ordered to throw into the trench. So, covered with shoes, she lay there till nightfall, till she heard the perpetrators leave, then crawled into the forest. Astonishingly, with the help of a few brave and kindly people, she managed to survive, first there, then back in town, for four years until the Red Army liberated Latvia, and the war was over. Her courage and resilience were extraordinary. As she had lived, she felt that God had chosen her to be a witness.

Here is the silence of the grave. Death. Night. Eternity.
Remember...
I swear to you:

I will tell them, the living, everything — everything
that I saw — who killed you and who betrayed you ...
I was with you at the executioner's block till the last
minute. Your blood flows in my veins, and your ashes
throb in my heart. (Michelson, 13)

The whole exercise was planned meticulously, with engineers
calculating the most efficient depth to which the pits should be
dug. Maybe this careful planning, the reduction of atrocity to
logistics, was a way to manage any human feelings that arose.
For the reality of the acts themselves there are no words.

It was in the British Library that I first read a description of
the massacre. As I sat there, it was not until I heard the call for
a two-minute silence that I realised that it was 11 November,
Armistice Day.

No silent remembrance can be long enough.

* * *

Although Nazi perpetrators, tried for war crimes at the Riga
trial held by the Soviet authorities in 1946, were found guilty
and hanged for their crimes, many of those responsible escaped
justice, including, notoriously, the man who became known
as the Butcher of Riga, Herberts Cukurs, deputy commander
of the Arajs Kommando. Although Cukurs never stood trial,
multiple Holocaust survivors' accounts credibly link him to war
crimes and crimes against humanity. Finally, in 1965, he was
assassinated by Mossad.

There is no doubt that many Latvians collaborated in the
murder of the Jews. According to historians, some were eager
volunteers. "It is a fact that Latvians were taking part in the
Jewish killing," said Vilis Daudzins. "...There are things we
don't like to talk about." (*The Guardian*, 16 March 2010). At a
Holocaust Remembrance conference in Stockholm in 2006,

Latvian president Vaira Vike-Freiberga said that the "precise number" of Latvians who participated in the mass murder of Jews was "not known but was estimated to exceed 1,000". As three survivors testified, that participation included those complicit in the Rumbula shootings.

But, despite the fact that several of the perpetrators were explicitly identified in eyewitness accounts, "Researchers studying the role of Latvian paramilitary units assisting the Nazis in murdering Jews note that no collaborator from the Latvian SD Auxiliary Security Police or Latvian police battalions was ever convicted by Latvian authorities." ((https://yated. com/holocaust-restitution-bill-evokes-bitter-history-of-latvias-jews/)

And Riga now, eighty years on?

Mike, a Western visitor who has visited Riga many times in recent years accompanied by a Latvian speaker, likes the city. He finds it vibrant, full of energy, culturally diverse, multi-lingual, and full of artists and musicians — much as it might have been before the war. The relationship of Latvians with their history, he says, seems to be that for most of the population the Nazi years were less bad than the ones under Soviet domination, when all Latvian property was nationalised, and hundreds of thousands of Latvians were murdered or sent to Siberia. Unlike the Soviets, people say, the Germans did not try to stamp out the Latvian culture. Indeed, when the Nazis drove out the Red Army in 1941, the Germans were seen by many as liberators, and Nazi propaganda had persuaded Latvians to believe that the Jews were in league with the communists.

In any case, some modern Latvians seem to be less concerned about what the Germans did to a minority like the Jews than Stalin who, in much more recent memory, fresher in their minds, tried to wipe Latvia off the map. And this neighbouring threat, so much nearer, has not gone away. The distance between Moscow and Riga is less than 1000 kilometres; many say that only Latvia's involvement in the EU and NATO helps to protect them.

The Latvian dislike of the Soviets extends to the Russian speakers in their own land. Most have come from various parts of the Soviet Union since the Second World War, but the suspicion extends even to those who are Latvian born and bred. And that includes the few Jews, Russian speakers, who still live there. In 1925 there were over 95,000 Jews in Latvia; according to the 2021 census, there are now about 9,000, most of whom live in or around Riga, and three-quarters of whom are Latvian citizens.

The dislike of Russia, Mike feels, helps Latvians absolve themselves of any responsibility for what happened to the Jews, or their part in it. But Frida Michelson's account makes no bones about the behaviour of "ordinary" Latvians. As soon as the Germans arrived, Latvians befriended them, girls went out with the soldiers; some took pleasure, it seemed, in pointing out the houses of Jews. Latvian police raped Jewish women, and in the ghettos and the days of killing, it was the Latvian police who were the enablers.

Michelson's sombre account, *I Survived Rumbali*, tells of a wholesale Latvian complicity in the treatment and subsequent murder of Jewish people, a complicity which the Soviet Union has subsequently denied. Not for nothing were her original Yiddish notes confiscated by the KGB. Even in its then guarded style, the book she finished in 1967 could not be published in Russia, but had to be passed round from person to person in secret. Only in the 1970s, after her migration to Israel, could she re-write her notes, find an English speaker to work with, and finally get the book, now written more frankly, published.

Reading Frida Michelson's extraordinary account was painful, It brought to life the details of what she, my grandmother, great-grandmother and great-uncle endured in a way that no overarching account can do. I read it on the day after Holocaust

Memorial Day in 2023, a year in which the theme was "Ordinary People". *I Survived Rumbali* is full of the stories of ordinary people: of the few courageous individuals who over the four years that Michelson was on the run gave her food, helped her, even sheltered her at risk of their lives, but also of the neighbours who stopped talking to her and the many, even those she knew, who shut the door in her face. What ordinary people did: both those who endangered their own lives by helping or sheltering a Jew, and those who were complicit. And the survivor account makes it clear that there were many of them: ordinary Latvians who joined in the oppression and massacre, either through fear, to appease their occupiers, or those who, perhaps influenced by Nazi propaganda, relished the opportunity.

Of course it is important to remember the magnitude, the monstrous scale of the atrocities of the Holocaust: the millions killed; the thousands herded into ghettos, humiliated, starved and shot on the day of my grandmother's death, but in being caught up in the numbers, seeing those individual people as a mass, is to succumb to a form of the dehumanisation that led their killers to behave as they did. By reading one woman's account, we can see the humanity in each of those individuals; we can begin to imagine the degradation of human life, to see the human soul in each of those individuals. To celebrate my grandmother's life is to see her beautiful soul rise from the floodgates of that butchery, and to give thanks for her legacy, the threads of her life in mine.

Paris, 1995: A different truth emerges

To celebrate my mother's eightieth birthday, as my mother had refused to go back to St Petersburg, she and I went instead to Paris to see my cousin sing Carmen at the opera house. We stayed in a small hotel and, probably for the first time since my teens, we shared a room. And in those four days, in our twin beds, we talked more and at greater depth than I could remember doing, and I found that some of the history of my mother's family as I had learnt and understood it over the years was wrong.

Maybe it was the emotion of the opera that moved her to open up; maybe it was just easier to speak when unseen, but in the dark, she began to speak with an intimacy that was rare. And even more unusually, she spoke of her father. I could hear her breathing and wondered how much these revelations were costing her, reliving something that rarely left her mind — her mother's fate, and her own inability to save her.

And her father. All my life she'd led us to believe that he had abandoned them. But that story turned out to be untrue. She, her mother and brother left St Petersburg after his disappearance, leaving him for dead. In fact, he was in a Bolshevik prison. And, although they could not be in touch, apparently Dora had known.

I asked why he had been imprisoned.

"He was wealthy, bourgeois, that's all." A pharmacist, he had bought and sold some patents that had made him rich.

"He turned up later, in Riga," my mother now said, "with another woman in tow. And another daughter."

Astounded, I turned to her in the darkness. "What? So you had a half-sister? Didn't you want to know what happened to her?"

"No," said my mother flatly. There could be no firmer negative. She never wanted to know. Not about her, nor about him. But her father had not abandoned them; it was they who had abandoned him. Hearing this now felt as if my mother had lied to me for all those years. But, on reflection, that was probably how it appeared to her, his disappearance concertinaed in her mind with the moment he turned up with another woman. Disappearance — betrayal. But, hiding for many months, caught, imprisoned again before escaping once more — I wonder how. He seems to have been something of a Houdini. And, to be fair, my mother can't have seen much of him. He must either have been away in the army or hiding for most of her early childhood. And then her parents parted, and she left with her mother for Switzerland.

Did Dmitri, perhaps justifiably, feel abandoned and free to make a new life for himself? He and Dora had married in 1914, just a year before my mother was born. Soon after Mischa was born in 1918, or even soon after he was conceived, Dmitri had had to disappear. So the couple had had very little time together. Had this new love been there for him at a time of great need? Or was it, as no doubt my mother would have said, simply a womaniser at work again? She told me that she lost touch with Dmitri in the Second World War (I had previously thought it was years earlier, but learned that as a teenager she had had tea with him). He had fought in two wars, been captured first by the Japanese, then by the Bolsheviks. He had managed to escape in both cases, but this time, in this, his third war, from the Nazis there was to be no escape.

Later I learned that when Dmitri caught up with his family in Riga, he asked for a divorce. After five years' separation, he and Dora were estranged, and he wanted to remarry. The couple did in fact divorce — such a rare thing at the time. He visited occasionally to see his children, although Mischa refused to see him. And, my mother said, her father had turned up during the war. And then — silence. There is no further trace, until records were found in Yad Vashem's Hall of Names, under the name Dmitrjs Zamuels Fisbergs. So he too died in the Shoah (Holocaust), probably in the same year as Dora. At any rate, as we were to discover some eighty years later, he had not lived to enjoy this new relationship for long. What was he doing in Riga? It was, after all, the home of his in-laws and his now ex-wife. Not his. Did he come there to see something of his children? Or was it by chance, just the place that many people went to after leaving St Petersburg? He was there on a refugee's temporary passport, with a visa that expired in 1932. So what happened after that?

Did Dmitri manage to remarry? And what happened to this woman? How long were they together? And her daughter, my mother's half-sister? There was no way of tracing either woman. Who knows who they were or what became of them. Long gone now, of course. We have never learned their names or their fate. All we have of the lives of these human beings are mere wisps of an old, now dead, woman's bitter memory.

The survivors

Of my grandmother's generation of our family, there were two survivors: Dora's cousin, Berthe, who ended up in Paris, and Dora's older sister, Becca, who lived most of her life in Switzerland. Both were remarkable women in their different ways. In 1912, Becca became the first woman in Switzerland to qualify as a doctor but, without Swiss citizenship, she was unable to practise. She also translated Dostoevsky and other Russian classics into German under the name Rebecca Candreia, publications that are still available, including a collection of Chekhov novellas with an afterword by Vladimir Nabokov. Like her mother, Paulina, she was a strong woman. When my uncle Mischa was in danger of being expelled from his Swiss grammar school, it was Becca who went to see the headmaster, his mother Dora, apparently, being too shy. Becca lived until 1972, when she was in her late nineties — given the chance, it's a long-lived family — and came to stay with us in London. I was too young to remember, but Eric remembers her well. He found her amusing, and quoted one of her favourite sayings: *"Schadenfreude ist die reinste freude"*. (Joy in another's misfortune is the purest joy.) One can see why people might have found her challenging.

"I got on with her," said Eric, "because she liked boys and didn't like girls. Mum was the opposite." He remembers Becca being ill when she stayed with us, and being told by the doctor not to eat any meat. She said, "Doctors (and she was one), they know nothing", ate meat and was promptly sick. My mother found her difficult and said Becca had bullied her when she was a child. One story goes that Becca's husband, Franz, fancied my mother, and Becca was jealous. And that Becca was fond of Mischa's first wife and would not relate to his second, Iranian, wife, Poury, to whom my mother became very close. Families!

Despite these stories, the very warm letters from Becca to my mother in the 1940s, including her response to the news of her forthcoming marriage to my father, show another side:

> I want to congratulate you and your little Eric with all my heart, and I am so happy at the thought of your happiness ... It's the only joy I've felt in so very long. I always wished you would know such happiness, and it came sooner than we ever thought.
>
> ...The thought that you are no longer alone, but instead have such a charming partner near you fills me with such joy.

Berthe was a very different character. Her son, Alec (always known to us as Lilik), said that Berthe was born in a Baltic state — I presume Latvia. In his memoir. *Without Drums or Trumpets*, which chronicles the extraordinary adventures and heroic acts of his wartime life, he says of his mother that she was brought up in St Petersburg "under the iron hand and strict surveillance of her mother, Ada, and a German governess".

> She had spent her youth reading avidly, devouring French books, and playing the piano. She was fluent in four languages, and educated well beyond the standards of a woman of her generation. The Russian Revolution stranded her in Stockholm where she promptly married a handsome young French lawyer with temporary diplomatic status without realising that he was as boring as he was erudite. (Le Vernoy, 166)

We are unsure of the exact relationship of Berthe to the rest of us. We always called her Tante Berthe, but we don't think her mother Ada was Dora's sister, but a cousin.

When Alec was born, they moved to France. They divorced in 1924, and Berthe remarried "a brilliant journalist and politician" who died in 1933. She and Alec had always been very close but they fell out when he insisted on signing up for the army. Later in the war, however, finding her German a considerable asset, she herself decided to join the Resistance.

At one point she had been arrested by the Gestapo and sent to Fresnes Central Prison where she had met many other women Resistance fighters, among them Genevieve de Gaulle. She had been questioned and left in prison for many months. She had known cold, misery and hunger. But one morning she had been set free — by mistake. (*ibid.*, 167)

Berthe lived into the 1970s, and she was the only member of that generation of my family that I remember. We visited her often in Paris in her smart 16th *arrondissement* apartment but until I read Alec's book, I had no idea of her involvement in the Resistance; she never spoke of it and I was astonished to hear it. I found it hard to reconcile this wartime heroism with the very elegant woman who on our first meeting pointed out a stain on my new and much-disliked suit. "*Tiens, tu as une tâche.*" As if I wasn't nervous enough already!

When I was about twelve, she came with my mother to visit me one Easter when I was staying on a farm near Blois on a school exchange. They were rather shocked at the primitive conditions, and tried to persuade me to leave.

She came to stay with us in England, and I remember on a hot summer's day playing bridge with her in the garden. I can't remember who else was playing. Possibly my father but certainly not my mother, who detested games of any sort, and despite her own earlier prowess in skiing and riding, could not see the point of sport. Tante Berthe claimed that she didn't speak English, so we played in French. I was partnering her and, wanting me to lead hearts, she said, gesturing across her heart: *"Tu me fends le coeur"* ("you're breaking my heart")! Although she lived in Paris for many decades and we always spoke French, I was surprised to discover that letters to my mother that I found from the 1950s are in German.

Our visits to Paris continued into the 1970s, including one with my children. My daughter remembers the chocolate cake.

The diaspora

'Never in the history of Europe has a political cataclysm torn such huge numbers of people from their mother country and from their homes'.

These words, written by Russian émigré journalist and politician Ariadna Tyrkova-Williams in December 1921 (British Library Add MS 54466, ff. 93-96), refer to the Revolution and civil war that tore Russia apart from 1917 until the early 1920s. The war led to the displacement of over one million people, including countless children. The majority of the refugees sympathised with the Whites, the group of forces who fought the Bolsheviks on a number of fronts across the country, and were from Russia's educated classes. Due to their political affiliation and the effects of war and famine, people chose, or were forced, to flee their homes as the Whites suffered heavier defeats. Those who could left Russia for Europe or the Far East. Tens of thousands initially fled to Constantinople before settling in the newly independent Baltic countries or cities such as London, Belgrade, Paris, and Berlin. (https://blogs.bl.uk/european/2015/12/ index.html#:~:text='Never%20in%20the%20history%20 of,Library%20Add%20MS%2054466%2C%20ff.)

Over a hundred years later, we have become horribly familiar with European refugee crises — not least from Ukraine after the Russian invasion in 2022.

My mother's family, like many others during the Second World War, was scattered, splintered. After her marriage, Genia was in frequent contact with her relations: keeping in touch, when it was possible, was something to be treasured, even if it took four months for letters to arrive. In letters from her uncles and aunts, we catch glimpses of how the war was affecting lives elsewhere. Writing in August and November 1943 from the safety of Switzerland, are letters from Becca and, on the other side of the almost translucent paper, in similarly tiny handwriting, from her husband Franz, as Genia called him (or, as he was writing in French, François). They were spending their holidays on the farm near Geneva belonging to Otto, one of Genia's first husband Felix's brothers, and he and his wife, Hilde, also contributed to the letters. Sharing their own family news, they express their delight at my mother's remarriage, and at the photo of little Eric, "so handsome" and looking content.

Hilde, who was working for the Red Cross, said how conscious they were of their privileged position.

We do all what we can to soothe the suffering we see. Alas! Many around us have taken in refugees, many of whom have been harshly faced with considerable losses of life.

They all write with great affection, Hilde signing her letter to her sister-in-law "*Je t'embrasse tendrement*" ("I kiss you tenderly"). News was hard to come by, but they tried to be optimistic, Otto writing: "I remain with the firm conviction that we shall see the return of better days, peace, justice and human dignity."

Dora is very much in their minds. Uncle Franz writes, "We haven't heard anything from your mother, alas." In the same bundle of letters, Becca writes:

> I spend my days in thought and in gratitude for all that is dear to me. It's still impossible to get in touch with your mother, but I know, I feel it, that we will see each other again, and we will do everything in our power to make her forget all her suffering.

And again, poignantly:

> I hope that we will soon have peace and that we will see each other, and I have the deep belief that your mother will be there with us, and I will be there to make her forget all her suffering.

None of them knew that Dora was already dead.

England, 1945–2017

My parents and Eric moved to England in 1945. The war was still on, and they travelled from Egypt in a troop ship — a two-week journey of some danger from the still-present U-boats. Eric, as a small child, found the journey highly enjoyable, but when, after the sunshine and blue skies of Egypt, they arrived in a cold and drizzly Liverpool, he wondered why they had come! They were met by my father's brother, Francis, in naval uniform, and stayed initially with my father's parents, before taking a flat in Buckingham, where Eric went to an English school for the first time. This was my mother's first visit to England, and her first meeting with her in-laws.

After some months, my parents moved to a flat in Hampstead, London. For my mother the culture shock of London life was considerable. Used to the relative luxuries of living in Cairo, with its lively social life and the availability of a wide range of delicacies, coming to a city with extensive bomb damage, and a country restricted by rationing, was a hard transition. As a beautiful woman who dressed smartly, she made a conspicuous figure among a population that had suffered greatly during the war. She told a story of how in her early days in London she arranged to meet my father for lunch. Walking through Soho, she wanted to ask the way, and chose a well-dressed woman who tucked her arm in her own, and said "Come with me, ducky," or words to that effect. My father was aghast to see his wife and an obvious prostitute walking arm in arm down the street towards him. My mother felt ill at ease, a foreigner and a Jew at a time when in England too antisemitism was rife. Although Eric said they were always very kind, Genia told me that even with her in-laws she felt out of place.

My mother's complicated history brought extensive bureaucratic difficulties. There was some confusion about her actual date of birth. When she was born, Russia was still using the Julian calendar, which differed by thirteen days from the Gregorian one, used elsewhere. (This is why the Russian Revolution of 7 November 1917 New Style is known as the October Revolution, because it began on 25 October Old Style.) In many countries both calendars were used simultaneously, so dates in the transition period until the changeover in February 1918 are often ambiguous. My mother celebrated her birthday on 19th January; in her Swiss passport used in the 1940s, her birth date is given as 6 January 1915. This does not explain the greater discrepancy on her birth certificate of a birthdate of 1916. For many years, she liked the idea of being younger, until she came up to pension age, when she wanted very much to prove her earlier birthdate! We don't know where the birth certificate was registered — she presumably had no papers from Russia.

After the turbulence of the first thirty years of my mother's life, her life in England was at last more settled. Once the Second World War was over, for the first time since her teens, she was living in peace. There were of course difficulties: getting used to life in another country yet again: new people, a different language, a different culture, but she did not have to live in fear. She and my father were in love and happy.

And they made good and, in some cases, lifelong friends with those living nearby. Eric and I played with the children of neighbours; I sailed my little boats on the White Stone Pond in Hampstead, as my own children were to do later.

But in 1951 things changed. When the war ended, my father had refused to take a permanent job in Military Intelligence, and had joined the civil service. He applied initially to join the Foreign Office, but was refused because of my mother's Russian nationality. He joined the Colonial Office instead, travelling extensively, and rising to the post of Principal at a very young age. At the age of 33, he was sent to Malaya to gain more experience, as a District Officer in Province Wellesley. I and my mother followed him a year later and lived there for a year before coming home; he followed later. My brother, aged 13, was left behind in England to take his Common Entrance exams.

This was the time of the Emergency in Malaya: an uprising led by the Malayan National Liberation Army (MNLA), the armed wing of the Malayan Communist Party (MCP) rebelling against colonial rule. As workers' houses were burnt, rubber plantations attacked and trains derailed, my father was in the thick of it, often going out into the jungle in the early hours of the morning. By then, General Sir Gerald Templer had taken over as High Commissioner, and shifted the emphasis from a brutal military approach to winning the hearts and minds of local people.

I remember many years later seeing on the door of the little box room of our London home a reminder of that time — a Wanted poster. All those names and faces of Chinese guerrillas: young men, boys, really. In our peaceful suburban home so many years later, it was an unsettling reminder of another world.

For my mother, the Malay experience was also a brief reprise of colonial life. She once again lived a genteel existence, with servants; she taught sewing and did first aid for the villagers; we had a cook and I was cared for by an *amah*. We lived in a beautiful large white house on stilts, of which we still have photos, in a village (now a city) near Penang called Bukit Mertajam. Once again my mother's sensitivity was apparent: she felt the house was haunted. She had a powerful experience of a ghostly presence. One night she felt an iron grip on her shoulder, with a profound sense of evil against which she knew she had to fight with all her might. We learned later that a young woman had been murdered in the house by a ship's captain.

There was a tennis court, and my parents played, even in the extreme tropical heat, taking salt tablets to prevent dehydration. I remember little of that time, except a friendship with the Tamil cook. At five years old, I was a confident child; I had a tendency when told things to say decidedly, "I know", whereupon Cookie would say "Jennetpa (his version of my name) knows everything" — a saying that has passed into family lore.

And of course, I remember the accident. Borrowing a tricycle from another little girl, I set off down the hill and found the brakes didn't work. To the horror of my mother and other onlookers, I shot over a crossroads, narrowly missing a car, and flew over a low wall at the bottom of the hill into a garage forecourt. People came running down the hill, but my mother told me that it wasn't her that I had cried for, but my father. She never forgot it: her hurt went deep.

I had broken my leg, and spent many weeks with it up on a chair, listening to 78 records of classical music. I still remember some of them: Mozart's *Eine Kleine Nacht Musik* and *Andante for flute and orchestra*, and a choral work in Spanish. I can't remember the name of it. but could hum it to you. Like my mother, who once sang to me a lullaby in Russian that her mother had sung to her, my aural memory is strong.

We travelled to Malaya by ship. It was a six-week sea voyage. Although I don't remember much of our journey, I remember sliding on my bottom along the deck during some rough weather, and I've been told — and there are photos of me wearing an officer's cap — that I was the only child on board ship, and "spoilt rotten". Especially at Christmas. I obviously wrote to Father Christmas, because I still have the telegram — we had them in those days — purporting to be from Father Christmas, acknowledging my request. Dated 24.12.52, from "North Pole Radio", the message reads: *TOO FAR TO BRING A WALKIE-TALKIE DOLL BUT WILL BRING WHAT I CAN* signed, *FATHER CHRISTMAS.*

On our return to England, my mother and I lived for a few months with my father's parents, who had moved to the seaside resort of Folkestone, where I went to school. Having been abroad, I was a bit behind in my studies, and worried about doing subtraction for the first time. We lived independently, with a little gas ring to cook on, and had access to a multitude, a feast, of books, including bound copies of nineteenth-century editions of the *Strand* magazine, some of which I inherited, including the first publications of the Sherlock Holmes stories. It was a place to which I returned for many of my school holidays: a secure place with set and settling routines for a girl whose home life was often chaotic.

We then moved back to London and, joined by my brother, now fourteen, lived for six months in a hotel in Finsbury Park. It was the time of the coronation, which we watched with staff and other residents on the hotel's new-fangled black and white television. A great excitement and a completely new experience for us all.

When my father finally returned from Malaya, we moved into a spacious semi-detached house in the London suburb of Golders Green, where I was brought up and my mother remained for the rest of her life. But our lives were far from settled. On my father's return to England came an unsettling reminder of the uncertainties of my mother's earlier life. My father had a mental breakdown. The immediate cause would seem to have been the stress and loneliness of his position in Malaya, but it went a good deal deeper. He was diagnosed with schizophrenia and suffered from it for the rest of his life. My mother cared for him; he had many spells in psychiatric hospitals, and for much of his life was affected by the prescribed drugs.

So my mother's life in London, although without war or revolution, was still a very taxing one. She told me that Dad was the love of her life; that she felt she had met him in a previous life. Letters he wrote from Malaya, and later during a period of lucidity on a trip to New York as part of the UK delegation to the United Nations, show the closeness of their bond.

> My dearest little sweet...
> All my love and lots and lots of kisses from your very own E.

To see her beloved husband descend into paranoia and madness was a terrible thing. In the early days, she felt very lonely and out of her depth. Dealing with psychiatric social workers and sometimes police; trying to get him into hospital as he took a turn for the worse in the middle of the night — she didn't know how things worked in England and wished that my father's family — English, after all — could have been more helpful. Like her mother before her, she had to cope on her own with two small children.

She had not only to care for her husband — and did so for about forty years until the last few years of his life, when she could not manage to lift him if he fell — but to earn a living. When he lost his civil service job, there was considerable worry that we would lose our home, but in the end, the civil service paid off the mortgage, so at least our housing was secure.

Family life

Despite this unpredictability, my mother and — when he was well enough — my father built a stable and loving home for us all. My mother joined a writing group, made friends with neighbours, and studied pottery, which was to become a mainstay of her life. We lived at no. 9; at no 1 was a couple who also did pottery and became firm friends; in later years I used to babysit for their son. At no. 3 was my piano teacher and her Austrian woman companion, whose fruit soup was a delight; at no 5 three elderly sisters, daughters of a vicar; at no 7 a rather grumpy elderly German Jewish woman, and on the other side of us, at no 11, a series of different people, including a family of Anglo-Indians. As a child, I was agog at the photo the father showed us of himself as the strongest man of India, with a lorry on his chest!

In the general neighbourhood of Temple Fortune too, my mother was a familiar figure. Living in the area for so long, she was well known and on very friendly terms with many of the shopkeepers.

My mother enjoyed making her own clothes — I remember the patterns were stored in an antique coal scuttle, still in the family — and despite my protests, she made clothes for me. She was a skilled knitter, which she did fast and in the continental way. She tried to teach me, but it was never something I wanted to do or was good at. When I was small, and we were short of cash, she knitted me a red swimming costume, which to my huge embarrassment sagged when I went into the sea.

I walked to a local primary school, then travelled a bit further afield to grammar school, where I became a prefect, then head girl. My mother took me to ballet and I studied piano with the teacher at number 3. I didn't get a piano or lessons until I was thirteen — too late to be any good. I wanted to learn specifically so that I could accompany my singing, but never managed to do both at once. I got to about grade six, but refused to take exams, which I always disliked, and of which I had enough at school. I did ballet from the age of five to thirteen, indeed went on Saturdays to a professional ballet school. We went to the Royal Ballet; I read books on famous dancers: ballet was in my blood. I wanted to be a dancer until puberty showed that I would be the wrong shape.

Hampstead Garden Suburb, just across the Finchley Road from where we lived, was a centre for many of my mother's and my activities. For my mother, pottery, and some teaching. For me, girl guides, church choir, and the amateur dramatic society, in which I became heavily involved. At the age of fourteen, I played the lead role of an eighteen year old, and I remember one of the women in the society having to take me aside to show me how to kiss!

I was a happy child; despite my father's illness, I knew that I was loved. The activities that my father and I did together felt precious, because they were so rare. He gave me his stamp collection, and took an interest in mine; we had a separate album for stamps from Ghana and Malaya — of special interest for him, since he had been to, worked in, both countries. He and I sometimes played tennis in courts in a nearby park. Although my love of reading came from both parents, it was from my father that I learned about English literature; the books I read in my early teens — adventure stories such as Rider Haggard and John Buchan — were influenced by my father's suggestions. My father was a historian and had an incredible memory: both inherited by my son, certainly not by me!

Neither of my parents learned to drive. We didn't have a car when I was growing up, except for a year or so during our time in Malaya, when my father did have, and drive, a Ford Prefect. We didn't have a television either. As a child, I used to sneak next door after school to watch programmes at a neighbour's. Although my mother would have liked a dog — she had had one as a child, and her brother always had them — we never did, although my brother made up for that in later life. As a child, I did, however, have a pretty tawny stripey cat, otherwise known as Katski, of which I was very fond. One day it scratched my mother and, to my horror, she gave it away without asking or even telling me, saying it was dangerous, might have scratched my face. I missed my little cat, and found it hard to forgive her.

My mother became something of a *mater familias*. Her spacious house became the focus of family gatherings, including an annual visit from my cousins on my father's side. On one occasion, when all partners and children were present, we numbered seventeen. My mother was an excellent cook, and I learned a lot from helping her. It was a great shame that in her last years she couldn't remember her recipes, couldn't even remember making them. She loved chocolate — in fact anything sweet — and a glass of wine, after which she could get quite giggly. "Why drink water," she would say, "if you can have wine?" I can remember an occasion, as an easily embarrassed teenager, when travelling with my rather tipsy mother on a bus, I moved seats to pretend we weren't together!

Altogether, she took great pleasure in good food and wine. Although she didn't talk about the food she enjoyed as a child, when I was growing up she did cook some Russian specialities, such as *borscht* and *piroshki* (little savoury pastries). And every Easter the wonderful heart-attack-on-a-plate *pascha,* a cake made from eggs, sugar, cream, almonds, and curd cheese, drained through muslin in a flower pot, turned out the next day and decorated with chocolate Easter eggs. It's a tradition that I and my children have continued to follow.

Having spent most of her life on the Continent, my mother's cooking was influenced especially by the French, and it was rare that a meal was not accompanied by salad. Very different from the English cooking provided by my schoolfriends' parents. She loved smoked salmon, always a mainstay of our Christmas meals. And for breakfast, long before muesli made its way into the British way of life, we would often have the original Swiss *bircher müsli*, made with grated apple and one other fruit per person. Right until the end she would have a glass of wine with her evening meal, and a few squares of dark chocolate.

We had biscuits sometimes at the end of a meal, but, having been brought up on the Continent, my mother didn't do puddings, and my father craved the stodgy puddings of his boarding school youth. The one benefit of his going to a nursing home at the end of his life was that at last he got treacle sponge and spotted dick!

Christmas was a festive occasion with us children and the grandchildren, and sometimes a friend of my parents who would otherwise be on her own, with several of us staying overnight. My mother was, however, never very keen on babies, only taking an interest when children were old enough to converse. As a child, I was allowed to stay up for adult dinner parties. The exposure to interesting adult company was a great richness, and a continental habit for which I'll always be grateful. I'm not sure if the guests treasured the experience!

As she got older, my mother took increasing pleasure in her little garden, and developed very green fingers. She hung a wind chime from the branch of a tree, and placed a large bronze Buddha on the ground. Having a spacious house was important when, for instance, my brother broke his leg in a motorbike accident in his twenties, and was able to come back home and rest up while it mended. At a later stage of my life, when I and my children were between houses, we came to stay for six weeks. I wasn't completely welcome, as my cousin from Switzerland, of whom my mother was very fond, came to stay at the same time. The last straw for my mother was the fact that we brought our little cat (another cat!), together with her litter tray. My father had one of his mini-strokes soon after we were there, and my mother remarked afterwards: "Don't worry, it wasn't your being there that caused it."!

During my childhood, holidays were rare events. A combination of shortage of money and the uncertainty of my father's condition made them problematic. The one I do remember was a trip in my early teens with my parents and a family friend to northern Italy: to the Cinque Terre and Nervi, such a lovely part of the world. We stayed in a family *pensione —*

something I was to do many times as an adult with my own family — and enjoyed the wonderful cooking of our hosts.

However, during our time there, my father became progressively more unwell, until we knew we had to return. The journey back by train, sitting up through the night, with my father talking loudly and disturbingly, was an unforgettably upsetting experience.

I went often to stay with my father's parents in Folkestone; my mother took trips on her own to France, sometimes to visit Tante Berthe in Paris, and once, in her late fifties, to the south of France — to Aix-en-Provence to study French literature. She returned refreshed and tanned, beautiful.

With a foreign mother and a father suffering from mental illness. I had little idea of where I fitted in. Had Dad been well, it would have been easy — I would have been part of a recognisable educated and privileged middle class — but, as it was, many of his friends fell away. Mental illness was a considerable stigma, even more than now. At school I made friends with another girl whose father had been diagnosed with schizophrenia: we found comfort in the other's understanding. But, when her father committed suicide, our friendship lapsed. She couldn't bear the fact that my father was still alive.

Solitude

As a family, we are used to being alone and, indeed, have come to need and value periods of solitude. We don't know how much Dora sought solitude, but there are few occupations as solitary as that of a concert pianist. One of the most enduring of my mother's memories of her mother is of her spending hours every day playing the piano — alone.

I spent a great deal of time alone as a child, and it's something that as an adult I find very important. But I am not an introvert, and need stimulus too. Finding the balance between the two is always a challenge.

I was ten when my brother went away to university, so I spent a good deal of time alone, listening to the radio, doing homework at the kitchen table, while my mother was teaching evening classes, and my father was in hospital. I may have been a bit lonely, but on the whole I enjoyed those peaceful times alone — a good grounding for what became a more contemplative way of life later on.

Solitude is of course different from loneliness, from feeling the absence of a parent or partner. I realise that all three of us — Dora, my mother and I — have spent many years living alone or without a partner. Dora, in all her life, had a mere three years with her husband. I hope she had friends. For my mother and myself, friendship has been a profound richness.

When my father moved into a care home and then died in 1996 at the age of seventy-eight, my mother lived, mostly contentedly, alone for another twenty years. Although her oldest friends, those of her own generation, had mostly died, she was a woman with a gift for friendship and had many younger friends. She continued with her pottery, and, astonishingly, in her eighties she became a Reiki master.

It was only in the last five years or so of her life, as my mother became frailer, that the need for outside care arose. My nephew moved in, and we employed carers to look after her.

In general, my mother enjoyed extraordinarily good health. Apart from a couple of bouts of jaundice, in childhood and in middle age, she was hardly ever ill. She did not get arthritis; she hardly broke a bone. When she was older, she suffered from essential tremor, which affected not only her hands but her speech. Coupled with her accent, it sometimes made her hard to understand, including in the recording of our interview. But, even in her nineties, when I accompanied her to hospital after a fall, when the nurse asked her if she had brought her medications, she was able to reply: "I don't have any."

Russia

Dora in Russia

Dora and Dmitri's marriage document

Sasha

Switzerland

Genia and her classmates at Chur, 1924

Haldenstein Castle

Genia in her teens   And later, Mischa, Swiss citizen

Egypt

Genia and Felix

Genia and "little" Eric

Genia and her husband, Eric

Wartime

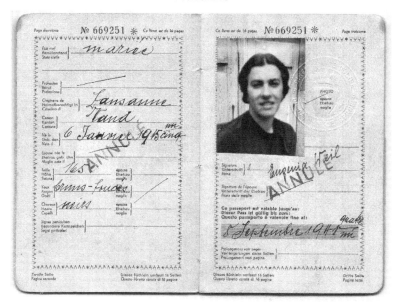

First page of Genia's passport

Swastika stamp on Genia's passport

Lilik in the British army

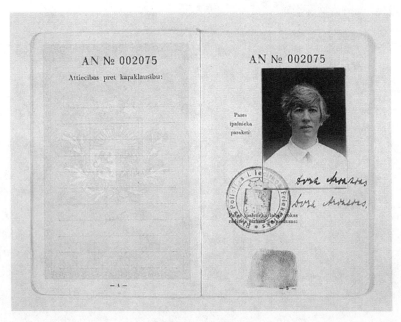

Dora's passport

Dmitri's passport

England

Jennifer and "little" Eric, 1950s

Genia and her husband, Eric, 1980s

Genia at 90

Part 2

Threads: The Legacy

Somehow in the depths I feel that life is continuous through the grave. It is like a stitch of embroidery which appears above the canvas, runs along and is seen, then dips back below out of sight. The thread, the wool, is continuous and only appears to disappear. Indeed, I had a strong feeling that only humans need starts and finishes, beginnings and endings. In the real spiritual world there are no starts and ends, all space, time and life are boundless and eternal. (Peter Tatton-Brown, *Quaker Faith & Practice*, 1989)

A woman's place…

The twentieth century, spanning the lives of Dora and Genia, was a time of radical change for the rights of women. Although, actually, women's suffrage, such a major issue in the UK, was slow to come to many countries, especially my mother's beloved adopted country, Switzerland, where women's right to vote was not approved until 1971. With a Swiss passport until 1941, Genia was not able to vote until she married my father and acquired British citizenship. Ironically, the Russian Revolution had led to much greater equality for women there, and in 1917 to Russia being the first of the major powers to grant women the right to vote. In fact, their passports record that in the 1920s both Paulina and Dora voted in Riga several times for both the national and local elections. Many years before their daughter and granddaughter were able to do so!

Russia under the Bolsheviks was in fact way ahead of other countries in establishing women's rights more generally. In 1918 they passed decrees on labour, marriage and the family, giving women the right to divorce, and establishing equality within marriage as well as equal pay. As more women entered the industrial workforce, State-run nurseries were provided free of charge. In 1920, Russia was the first country to legalise abortion. Oral contraceptives were in any case unavailable at the time, and other methods unreliable, so it became almost the only method of prevention.

Even though rights in many countries were now open to women, they were still living through a time of war and revolution, which demanded resilience from its citizens and meant that extraordinary choices had to be made. And, for much of the time, even for those privileged in class and financial position, social norms dictated constraints on women's freedom of choice.

Women's names carried a male imprint. In Russia, the middle name of a child was, and still is, a patronymic, formed from the first name of the child's father. My mother relates how, as a child of three or four, when a guest arrived in their flat, she proudly introduced herself as Evgenia Dmitriyovna Fischberg! On marriage, women in many countries took their husband's names, and still do. In the US, the figure in 2020 was around 70%, and in the UK, according to a 2016 survey, the figure is almost 90%. (www.bbc.com/worklife)

The practice was kept in our family. My grandmother was Aronson: on her marriage, her name was changed to Fischberg; my mother, married twice, changed her name from Fischberg to first Weil then Hanrott. When I married in 1970, it never occurred to me to keep my maiden name, although it would have been possible. After my divorce, I decided to stay with a name that I had had for longer than my maiden name. It was, after all, the name of my literary agency, and later, as a writer, the name on my books. There didn't seem to be much of a feminist reason for changing it: the name — whether of father or husband — is still that of a man! Interestingly, a post-marriage partner of some six years hated the fact that I bore the name of "another man". Had we married, I decided I would take his name, as a gift to him.

Others make other choices; many combine their surnames, and I have one friend who took his wife's name. I was touched by a bride's speech explaining her decision to take her husband's name. Her choices were to keep her own, to combine their names, for her husband to take hers or for her to take his. She said that since she now had a stepson, and he had his father's name, she had decided to join them. But it was a choice.

And up to and during the twentieth century most women followed their husbands to their homes or places of work. Dora moved to St Petersburg from Riga; Genia from Switzerland first to Egypt, and then to England, with a period in Malaya, when my father was sent there for work. And I followed my husband first to Wiltshire, when he worked in Swindon, and then to the Midlands when he worked in Birmingham. As I had opted to stay at home with the children until they were at school, we had to go where the money was. Once I started working in London, we did eventually move there.

It is extraordinary, therefore, to see how even a hundred years ago some of the women in my family surmounted the expectations of social norms. The example was set at the end of the nineteenth century by Paulina, my great-grandmother, who, with a husband more committed to his devotional life at the synagogue than to work responsibilities, had to take charge not only of the household but of the family business. She needed to be tough, and was apparently not someone to oppose lightly. The story goes that one teatime, when Dora said something she found irritating, she threw the teapot at her. My impression of their two daughters — and it is only an impression, as one died before I was born and I don't remember the other — is that they could not have been more different. Dora, by all accounts, was a gentle artistic character in a family of strong women; her sister Becca, like their mother, was tough.

Both sisters qualified to a high degree — Dora as a concert pianist; Becca as a doctor and a translator. It says a great deal for the parents' love for their daughters, and the importance they attached to women's education, that they were willing to give them such remarkable opportunities. But although both sisters were given these chances, neither was able to practise their chosen professions. Despite being accepted by and being allowed to travel to the prestigious Brussels Conservatoire to study music, Dora only performed in charity concerts; Becca was never able to practise as a doctor.

Their cousin Berthe showed her mettle in the Second World War, when despite initial hesitation, she joined the Resistance. Genia, my mother, never wanted to work, but circumstances demanded that she ended up having to do so. Life forced her into a more proactive role, first as a single mother in Cairo, then in later life when my father's illness forced her to earn a living. Although she may have found her work during the war fulfilling, she didn't like working when she was older, never wished to do it, and couldn't understand my eagerness to return to work when my children went to school.

I grew up in the 1960s, a time when much of Europe and America were caught up in not only political protest but social unrest, including the rise of the Women's Movement. Although I was aware of the inequalities suffered by many, I did not feel the need to get involved. I was lucky: unlike so many of my contemporaries I did not feel constrained by my gender. As my father's only child, he was happy for me to do whatever I wanted. At a girl's grammar school, the emphasis was on our studies and the kind of career we might want. I don't remember any emphasis on marriage or motherhood. Many of the girls were dating in their early teens. I found their preoccupation with boys rather silly; I was too focused on my studies. I was sixteen before I had my first boyfriend. I enjoyed school, and wanted to go to university — so there was no struggle on that front. Just a complaint from my mother that, with so many activities — music, hockey and a lot of acting both in school and outside — I was spreading myself too thin.

Motherhood

My mother's side of the family is a small one. Of course, so many were killed before I was born, but even of those who were left, Becca was childless, Berthe had one son. Dora had two children: a boy and a girl; my mother had two children: a boy and a girl, and so did I. My brother has a son and a stepdaughter, both of whom have children. Mischa had three children from two marriages, none of whom have children. I have one granddaughter. I married into a big family, and the contrast between their easy-going sociability and the spare intensity of ours was marked.

In my life, I have spent a great deal more time with my father's family, and know them much better than those on my mother's side. They are in England, after all. The scattered nature of what is left of my mother's family made and still makes it more difficult to see them, and means I know less of their lives.

Dora's death was not a subject that we discussed at home — my mother's guilt at not having saved her was palpable but under the surface. When she approached the age at which her mother died, she mentioned it; we could see that it had a powerful effect on her, but no more was said.

Although things change from one generation to another, we all learn how to parent from our own parents, On both sides of my family, both in England in Russia, the middle-class practices of the day were followed: by sending children away, and having others to care for them. As a small child, my mother had a nanny, to whom she was very close. Although I did not have a nanny — times were changing and in any case we did not have the money for it — when I was three or four my mother used to send me away to the seaside in Hove for my summer holidays to a woman she paid to look after me. And when we spent a year in Malaya a year later, my parents hired a local *amah* to look after me. For my parents, it was normal practice.

My father was sent away to boarding school at an early age. When I was thirteen my mother felt that with the difficulties at home, it would benefit me to go away. Although I got a scholarship to Wycombe Abbey, I refused to go: despite all the problems, I knew that I wanted to be at home, wanted to be part of the family. I never liked the idea of boarding schools and later, seeing the damage that it had done to my father, I never considered sending my children away. In the 1920s, my uncle

Mischa was sent away for his health to Switzerland, at the age of two. And it looks increasingly likely that a few years later, Dora left her children in Switzerland, in the care of her sister. Going to Riga, putting her parents first. During the war, my brother was sent from Egypt to Palestine for his safety at the age of three, and when we went to Malaya, he was left behind in England, the reason given being that he would not get a good education in Malaya, something he now says was unfounded. Staying partly in boarding schools, and partly with my father's family and family friends, it was a very unsettling time for him.

But on both sides too, parental obligation was strong, although not always caring. On my father's side, my great-grandmother lived with her daughter and husband, in her own little bedsit, where she ate her meals and apart from a daily teatime visit mostly sat alone. In the next generation, after my grandfather's death, my grandmother lived for half the year with each of her sons. My own mother was alone for many years after my father's death; I did not go to live with her and my own place was too small for the two of us. I also knew that we would have found it hard to live together. And as for my own older age, I do not have expectations of being looked after by my children; should I need one, I have my eye on a care home by the sea.

So, what do we know of motherhood on my mother's side of the family? That my great-grandmother was a hard taskmaster and not easy to live with; that, nonetheless, Dora left Switzerland for Riga to care for her in her old age, and some years later my mother left Egypt to visit them. Those decisions were to cost my grandmother her life, and my mother a narrow escape with hers. It is not surprising, then, that my mother's concept of motherhood was weighted with guilt and obligation. Having lost her own mother, she felt the mother-daughter bond to be a hugely important one.

And for first Dora, and then Genia, motherhood was for many years a solitary burden, and one to be borne in countries other than their own. When Dmitri was in hiding, and after their separation and divorce, Dora had to call on all of her reserves to look after her children first in St Petersburg, and then in Riga and Switzerland. And when her children left? Genia married early, at the age of 19, and went abroad; Mischa too went abroad soon after doing his Ph.D. How did Dora cope with the empty nest? Although she had relatives in Switzerland, they were mostly in other parts of the country. With no partner, she might well have felt lonely. Not surprising, really, that she spent so much time in Riga.

When Genia was widowed, she was of course alone, also in a foreign country and then, later, in England, when my father fell ill, she again had to take most of the responsibility for my brother and myself. Both my brother and I went to universities far from London — my brother to Liverpool and I to Leeds. I remember my mother being upset that I didn't want to stay at home and, even more so, after graduation, when I came to work in London, but took a bedsit rather than coming back to my childhood home. She was reliant on me, but I was growing up; I needed my independence. An empty nest is hard to deal with, and in my turn I found it so too. As with Dora, one by one they leave: the husband, the daughter, and then the son. For one reason or another, the fathers in this story were absent.

In my generation, and in my very English circle in Leamington Spa, there were lively discussions about the question of childcare and when and if to return to work. Passions ran high, each needing to feel that their decision was right. Some of my friends opted not to go back to work, but to be full-time mothers until their children were adults. Others took statutory maternity pay and went back after a few months. With a perhaps unconscious reaction to the practice of my forebears, I felt strongly that I didn't want others to bring up my children, so opted to stay at home until my younger child went to school, and spent seven years at home. Even so, one of my friends berated me for not devoting longer to my children's care. I was just a couple of years into my career; the freelance work that I could do from home felt life-saving — I waited eagerly for the advent of the postman. Even so, I missed my colleagues as well as family and friends, and became depressed, which wasn't good for me or the baby.

For families, decisions then, and even more now, revolved around balancing the financial need to work, the cost of childcare, and the demands of a career. In my day it was almost entirely a decision for the mother. Although a few rare men did take on child care, it seemed a given that fathers would go out to work, which resulted in many of them seeing very little of their small children. Nowadays, the balance is better with more fathers able to enjoy more time with their children. I am often moved by the sight of a dad interacting with a small child.

So the me part of this motherhood thread? Maybe it's only something that can be recognised in hindsight. Maybe it will be for my children and grandchildren to evaluate it; see what part of the cloth my life and being represent. And for the next generation, child-centred parenting is a far cry from the practices of previous generations!

But for me, now, I can say as a daughter, I was a good child. And growing up, unlike many of my contemporaries, some of whom joined the Greenham Common women's peace camp, I was strangely oblivious to political protest. I was brought up to believe in authority and, with the instability of mental illness in my family life, maybe I had a need for the stability that that brought.

For many years my mother and I were very close. She was protective of me as "a sensitive child". At the same time, it was made clear to me at an early age that my mother had had a very hard life, and that she needed me not to add to her difficulties. She needed my support. I did not have a teenage rebellion; I remember thinking I had nothing to rebel against: I felt so in tune with the love of the arts, the awareness of beauty, instilled in me at home. That is not to say that we never disagreed. My mother, for instance, did not always understand why I felt so strongly about equality and justice, particularly racism. I remember my mother saying, "I wish you'd stop going on about it. Anyone would think" — then I don't remember the rest, something like "you were one of them". In the way of many of her generation, she was casually racist in the "they're very good at dancing" kind of way, but would have been shocked at being thought so.

With my father often in hospital and my brother a lot older than me, my mother and I spent a lot of time alone together. When I was small, coming back from Malaya on the ship and the weeks spent in Folkestone before my brother, then my father, joined us. Later on, as I was growing up, Eric was first away at university, then married.

It was not until my marriage broke up when I was forty that I realised that the relationship with my mother was overwhelming. Her extreme empathy led often to the emphasis being not on what was going on for me, but on her response to it. I realised that I needed to distance myself. I don't think my mother ever came to terms with that shift in me. I realised too, as I found a spiritual home with Quakers, that I had accepted a lot that I now found unacceptable: a hierarchical society with authority largely unquestioned; the casual racism of some the books I'd read, such as John Buchan.

I remember my mother coming round to my small flat, soon after I'd moved in. I'd got rid of a lot of my possessions, and had little on the walls, wanting to avoid unnecessary distraction from being in the moment. She looked round at the almost empty walls and said, with sad disapproval, "Oh, you have changed." "Yes, Mum, I have changed." I have also become a vegetarian and, probably as a reaction to my husband's drinking, largely given up alcohol, though in my love of chocolate I am still my mother's daughter.

People do change and develop. It is easy for our own view of others to be stuck in time. Memory can be static. Never having met Dora, my image of her is stuck in the little photo I have of her and the idealised figure as portrayed by my mother, stuck in the romantic beauty of the young Dora. How she must have changed from a gentle young musician to a mother fighting for her children, fighting for her life. Maybe we had a need for that image to be stuck, to avoid imagining how she must have had to change to face the appalling years culminating in her death.

I was well aware of the changes in my mother. She too had been a romantic young woman, and in her early years of widowhood a flirtatious one. Years of caring for my father demonstrated an inner strength and resilience in later life, and eventually in old age a weariness took her over. We continued to see a lot of each other — I visited her weekly for about thirty years, except when I was away. As her eyesight diminished, I read each of my books to her. She loyally came to all my book launches: it meant a lot to me to have her support my writing. But I did realise that her support was conditional — she only approved of activities that were in tune with her own tastes, of a me that was in her own image. There was a judgmental side to her that I have struggled with in myself.

The Jewish thread

A female fetus is born with all the eggs she will ever have in her lifetime. So when your grandmother was carrying your mother in her womb, you were a tiny egg in your mother's ovaries. The three of you have been connected for a very long time. www. unravelbrainpower.com

It is from these basics of biology, suggests the Rebbe, Rabbi Menachem M. Schneerson, that Judaism has always passed through the female line.

An embryo must sit within its mother's womb and develop for nine months. During those months, the fetus is nurtured from the bloodstream of the mother, affected by her emotions, by the sounds she hears and the places she goes. And none of this, especially the birthing process, is a terribly comfortable experience for the mother.

This aside from the nursing and nurture, both physical and psychological, in the primary years that are most critical to the child's development. Generally, that's provided by the mother, who is capable of providing far more than the man.

Now, ask yourself, to whom would you give dominance in the fundamental identity of this child? https://www.chabad.org/)

* * *

In my grandparents' and mother's day, St Petersburg had a large Jewish population.

> By 1910, the number of legal Jewish residents had reached 35,000. Prior to the Soviet period, Jews never accounted for more than 3 percent of the city's population. But in such fields as banking, law, and journalism, they constituted as much as a third of the total number of professionals. Unlike other East European cities such as Warsaw, Kiev, and Odessa, Saint Petersburg was always dominated by a single ethnic group: Russians, who represented 80–90 percent of the population. Also unlike those cities, and because of a large police and army presence, the Russian capital never experienced a pogrom.
>
> Saint Petersburg never had a Jewish ghetto, and tsarist authorities were determined to prevent the formation of one. Nonetheless, the majority of Jews who moved there chose to settle in the Pod"iacheskii neighbourhood just south of Nevsky Prospekt, the city's grand central boulevard. Throughout the late imperial period, they remained one of the city's most residentially segregated ethnic groups. Yet the Jews of Saint Petersburg adopted Russian as their native language more quickly than any other ethnic minority...
>
> (https://yivoencyclopedia.org/article.aspx/saint_petersburg

Dora and Dmitri were part of that community but, like many others, were not practising Jews but, as far as we know, thoroughly assimilated into the large professional middle class of which they were also a part.

The relative fluidity, not to say chaos, of the first decade of Bolshevik rule opened a rather wide field for Jewish cultural and religious activity, invigorated by waves of immigrants to the former capital. Pre-revolutionary organizations ... continued their work, albeit under growing financial and ideological constraints. The newly founded Leningrad Jewish Religious Community ... served as an umbrella group for most of the city's two dozen synagogues and congregations. In 1918, a Jewish university was founded in Petrograd...

This was not to last.

By the end of the 1920s all independent Jewish institutions in the former capital had been shut down under suspicion of "bourgeois nationalism" and "religious obscurantism," part of a broader campaign of Bolshevik consolidation across the Soviet Union (*ibid.*).

* * *

Like her parents, my mother was never a practising Jew: not in Switzerland (where indeed she attended a Catholic convent), nor in Egypt, although her first husband was also Jewish, nor in England.

In 1954, my parents bought their first house. It was in the London suburb of Golders Green, an area renowned for its Jewish population — not something that my parents knew at the time. Many of our neighbours were Orthodox Jews, with large numbers of children. My mother did not feel in tune with the more tribal elements of her origins. She was, however, a great supporter of Israel, and was very upset at the Six Day War in 1967. "Poor little Israel," she would say, "surrounded by all those big countries." And I was convinced; that's how it felt at the time. Of course, since then the balance of power in the region has changed, as has my view of Israel's behaviour.

In her fifties, my mother discovered the Kabballah, the mystic side of Judaism, and her Kabballah group, run by the very respected teacher and writer, Warren Kenton, was a central part of her life and a source of joy for many years. It was left to my brother, Eric, to pick up the reins of Jewish practice, in his fifties becoming the first observant Jew in our family since our great-grandfather, Bernhard, whose name my brother bears as a middle name. Bernhard was, apparently, a highly respected member of the Jewish community, so the name seems entirely appropriate. Eric's sense of himself as a Jew, he says, came gradually, but when he went to a Saturday service, he had a sense of being in the right place.

I am a Jew, but I wasn't brought up in the Jewish faith. When I was growing up, my mother was a non-practising Jew; my father was an Anglican, so I was baptised, and later confirmed as an Anglican. I was quite a pious little girl; as my brother was an atheist at the time, from the age of five, when my father was converted to Roman Catholicism, I was the only Anglican in the family. At eighteen my faith went underground for many years, as I made a career and brought up a family. In my late forties, faith found me again, and I made a home with the Quakers. In spiritual matters, as a family we are, it seems, late developers! And, despite our different labels, I found myself very much alongside my parents in our mystic tendencies.

Apart from my mother's first marriage, none of the family in recent times have married Jews. Since the Jewish identity passes through the maternal line, I and my children are Jewish, as is my brother, but not his son. And not my son's daughter, born in 2020: so this branch of Judaism dies out with my children. In recent history, only men of our family have been practising Jews: my great-grandfather and my brother. None of the women have been, apart from my mother's late convincement to the Kabbalah.

My son told me recently that at my mother's funeral, her next-door neighbour, an orthodox rabbi to whom she was not close, took him aside and said: "I don't know about all this Quaker stuff, but remember you're a Jew."

During most of my life, I have not felt very Jewish. It was not something we talked about as I was growing up, and I have only a passing knowledge of the feast days and practices. There were, after all, no practising Jews in our family at the time. Since finding my own faith, however, I have felt drawn to writings from the mystic end of the faith: not the Kabbalah, which I find too complicated (and maybe I needed to find something separate from my mother's faith!), but to Hasidism in its early guises, notably its eighteenth-century founder, Baal Shem Tov, and Martin Buber, who was much influenced by early Hasidic thought. I can certainly relate to one of the movement's prime insights, as described by Buber (and quoted by Harvey Gillman in his book about being a Jewish Quaker, *A Minority of One*): "The Hasidic concept of the world was one of a world as it was in a particular moment of a person's life; a world ready to be a sacrament, ready to carry out a real act of redemption. The present moment is the moment of eternity" (49).

Despite this sense of kinship, even as I type I have a sense of something withheld, a questioning of the relevance of Judaism to my life. I did a double-take when a friend, knowing I was writing this book, referred to me as someone of Jewish heritage. Labelling myself in that way hasn't been the way I think of myself. Maybe, in writing this book, I am not only discovering an expanded sense of family, but growing into my Jewish identity.

But it's not a straightforward journey. I find it has induced an unwelcome self-consciousness, looking at people I meet, or pass in the street, and asking myself: "Is s/he Jewish?" It has never happened before. At a London book launch as part of Jewish Book Week, I was startled to be offered a Jewish Chronicle tote bag containing a copy of the paper. The venue's cafe had provided what they considered Jewish fare: smoked salmon and cream cheese bagels and salt beef sandwiches. As a vegetarian, I did not find them appealing. And I wondered how many visitors would respond well to a rather stereotypical offering. As usual, I imagine, there would be a spectrum of reaction.

I am a Jew, but I am also a Quaker. How is that? Sometimes the threads of connection are woven so fine as to take on the appearance of invisible mending. On the face of it, my spiritual home and my religious identity have little to do with my Jewish ancestry. But in fact there is no conflict; there are many Jewish Quakers. Recognising the riches that other faiths can bring, Quakers are happy to embrace people who are also Muslims, Buddhists or Jews; people from any other major faith, or none. Many come to Quakers from another faith or denomination and retain an affectionate loyalty for their former faith home. They are surprised, and relieved, to discover that there is no expectation that in coming to Quakers they have to cut off their connections with their previous affiliation.

That openness to other faiths was present at the very beginning of the Quaker movement. There is also a special connection between Jews and Quakers. In the seventeenth century, Margaret Fell, the "mother" of Quakers, was part of a movement to bring Jews back to England after their expulsion in the thirteenth century. With the beginning of an interest in Hebrew as a Scriptural subject some years before, a few Jews had been allowed in and by 1660, there was a small Jewish community in London. Margaret Fell wrote a number of letters to them. She reached out, believing that the Light was "shining on a new day for Israel as well as for England" (Bruyeel,166).

And in more recent times, on the eve of the Second World War, three American Quakers, including Rufus Jones, one of the founders of the American Friends Service Committee, made a trip to Nazi Germany to plead the cause of the Jews. He later wrote that he felt the visit had enabled the emigration of many Jews, and the extensive post-war relief, for which the Quakers won the 1947 Nobel Peace Prize.

And both Jews and Quakers have been persecuted groups. From its beginnings in the seventeenth century, the Religious Society of Friends (Quakers) suffered discrimination, persecution; in both the UK and the US, hundreds of its members were imprisoned, and some executed, for their unwillingness to conform. In the UK, university education was prohibited to "dissenters" until the late 19th century, barring them from professions that depended on a degree or conformity with the Church of England, leading many Quakers to work in the business sector. Like Jews, some of whom became much-derided moneylenders, Quakers founded many financial institutions and became known for their financial and business probity.

And both groups were prohibited from political careers. On July 26 1858, Lionel de Rothschild became the first Jew to take his seat in the House of Commons, after an eight-year battle, because of his refusal to take the Oath of Allegiance, until he was allowed to swear on the Old Testament with his head covered.

Quakers were barred from becoming MPs until the Corporation and Test Acts, which prevented Nonconformists from sitting and voting in the Commons, were repealed in 1828 and the first General Election after that was in 1830. That said, John Archdale, a Quaker, was elected to Parliament from the constituency of Wycombe in 1698 — but he couldn't take his seat because he wouldn't swear the required oath — and the absence of an alternative affirmation persisted until the 1880s.

A different aspect of exclusion led to Jews and Quakers being the only groups now allowed to perform their own marriages, with their own registering officers or marriage secretaries. The Marriage Act of 1753 explicitly exempted Quakers and Jews from the statutory regulation of all other marriages in England and Wales. It was intended to put a stop to what Lord Hardwicke and others saw as the "evil" of clandestine marriages — and the perceived remedy was to make everyone get married in a Church of England parish church. This was a serious matter for Jews and, less obviously, for Quakers. It was also a serious problem for C of E clergy, because they would have to marry Jews who, they knew, did not accept the divinity of Jesus, and Quakers whose position on the issue was possibly doubtful even then. Crucially, neither would agree to baptism. So as much to respect clergy consciences as anything else, the special provision for Jews and Quakers was put in the 1753 Act and has persisted ever since.

But whereas Quakers no longer suffer discrimination, antisemitism endures.

The connection between Jews and Quakers is not just in their history nor the external, organisational aspect of their faiths, but at a more profound level. As Andy Stoller, a Quaker brought up as an observant Jew, wrote on finding Quakers, there was

> a deeper, spiritual and cultural level that we recognised in one another.
>
> On the face of it, there is little in common between the two faiths. They sit at opposite ends of the Judaic-Christian spectrum ... Yet both are at their heart mystical religions, assuming the possibility of a direct relationship with God ... Both offer demanding guidance for the whole of life, not just for times of formal worship. My Jewish roots strengthen my belief that God is there to be talked with; being a Quaker has given me opportunities to deepen and grow my spiritual life, to explore my faith openly and take it forward. (The *Friend*, 25 Nov 2009)

And that mystic similarity was what I, as a Quaker, found in the Hasidim.

We don't know if Dora had a faith, although immersion in music, literature and art would be bound to foster and express a well-developed spiritual tendency. Her and my mother's devotion to and practice of the arts was not just as an escape from the grim realities of their lives, but stemmed from and resulted in an opening to a richer, more spiritual, dimension that strengthened their resilience. What is certain is that my parents and I shared a strongly mystical bent, that we shared what the Quaker Rufus Jones referred to as "the unnamed and unconscious mystical propensity" of his family.

We shared too an interest in other faiths: an openness to what faiths have in common at the mystic level. When my father died, we found a folder of cuttings on other faiths. Later in life, my mother was not only engaged in the Kabbalah, but also developed an interest in Hinduism, becoming friends with, if not an adherent of, a guru who from time to time visited London. I came across a battered old black and white postcard of "Sudama approaching the Golden City of Krishna", on the back of which my mother had written in her elegant handwriting:

May the five-pointed star of the Light of the Overself (soul) surround me and protect me and fill me with its radiance

with one attempted and one successful drawing of the star.

It is not just physical traits that can be inherited.

* * *

In an age when the concept of privilege is so much to the fore, there's no denying that my Russian family were part of the privileged elite, in reaction to which the Russian Revolution erupted. They were educated, affluent, and part of the professional middle, and, indeed officer, class. But they were also Jewish, subject to abuse and, in the end, to a brutal genocide. However assimilated, however little they practised their religion, that is how they were viewed by some, and treated accordingly. Like others, my Russian Jewish family had the best and the worst of both worlds. Both privileged and victims: the lot of many Jews throughout the ages.

> Culturally the Jew is seen both as "successful" and as "low class"; as capitalist and as "communist"; as "clannish" and as "intruding into other people's society"... as "strong" and as "weak"; as "magically omnipotent and omniscient, possessing demonical powers" and as being "incredibly helpless, defenceless — therefore readily attacked and destroyed". (Ackerman and Jahoda quoted in Dreizin, 2)

Antisemitism

I've never understood about antisemitism. According to Walter Laqueur in *The Changing Face of Antisemitism,* "Most Jews living outside Israel do not regard themselves as a people except by way of origin" (2). That is my experience. As a friend said of her mother: "She almost wouldn't have known she was Jewish if Hitler hadn't told her." The term "antisemitism" may only have been coined in 1879, but the fact of it has existed for centuries, and all over the world. Why? Why, over all those years, in so many countries, have the Jews been made the object of exclusion and hatred on such a vast scale? Why have individuals, families, a whole people, been subjected to such persistent vilification? As Laqueur asks: "What is different about Jews that may have attracted attack and persecution?" (1). Scapegoating is an ugly facet of human nature: to belittle, to view some people as "other". From viewing some as less human comes the ability to inflict ill treatment.

In the Middle East, Jews and Arabs, so akin ethnologically, have always found it hard to get on. Before Christianity, hostility towards Jews was just one of many national and ethnic antagonisms. After that, distrust and hatred towards the Jews led to extreme superstitions about Jewish attitudes and behaviour. A view by some Christians blaming the Jews for crucifying Jesus (even though he himself was a Jew) has led to allegations of the most extraordinary sort, such that Jews' supposed hatred of Christ leads them to poison Christians and their children. The "blood libel" accusation that Jews needed the blood of Christians for ritual ceremonies continued until the twentieth century. Jews were expelled from many countries, including from Britain in 1294, not being readmitted until 1655.

The antagonism towards Jews extends to vicious stereotyping, accusing them of being devious and disloyal, and ascribing to them negative physical characteristics such as hooked noses and an odious smell — nothing could be further from the truth when applied to the fine elegance of Dora and my mother.

Excluded from many professions, Jews found a niche in moneylending, which in itself demeaned them in others' eyes (think of Shylock), and led to systemic antisemitism, as Jews' success in financial dealings led to some of them becoming powerful, influential, in many societies. They were the subject of conspiracy theories and blamed both for assimilating and for keeping themselves separate. It is not surprising that many Jews have interiorised the abuse; absorbing the low esteem that others have of them. Some have left Judaism; others have an ambivalent attitude to their Jewishness, hiding or denying their Jewish identity. A friend said of her parents arriving in England after the war that all they wanted was a quiet life, to be invisible, not to be singled out in any way.

As Edmund de Waal wrote about Vienna and Paris in the 1890s: "Anti-Semitism was part of common day-to-day life ... It happened both overtly and covertly" (129). There were physical attacks, open abuse, and constant vilification in public and private life.

The special clothing and yellow stars of Nazi Germany were nothing new — as long ago as the Middle Ages, Jews were often made to wear special clothing or badges. Ghettos, with Jews restricted to certain parts of cities, also have a long history.

And anti-Jewish sentiments continue into the present day. Despite this, in the US, in the UK, even in supposedly liberal circles, Jews are still not considered a vulnerable group. In 2022, David Baddiel returned to the subject of his book, *Jews Don't Count,* in a TV documentary:

> "One of the points of the new documentary is that we Jews are a vulnerable community. And we are more vulnerable than people realise. Partly because they think that Jews are powerful. And I think the opposite."
> To demonstrate, in the new documentary he visits his old Jewish primary school, where the pupils take part in regular security drills. Like all Jewish schools and synagogues, entry points are protected by security. (*i* newspaper, 18 November 2022)

It is not surprising, perhaps, if some close-knit Jewish communities react with a defensive and insular attitude to others.

Despite their history of persecution, Baddiel says, in lists of persecuted minorities, including gay and trans people, Muslims, black people and people of colour etc., despite identity politics requiring a complete list, Jews are excluded. Somehow, they are seen as having privilege. Jews are attacked for being rich or poor, powerful or weak. Still caricatured today, open to ancient negative stereotypes.

My Russian heritage

If I've not felt particularly Jewish, the same could be said to be true of my relationship with my Russian heritage. Of course I've always been aware of the fact that I was half Russian — and as a child I rather revelled being endowed with such an air of exoticism. "My mother is Russian, you know." But what did the connection mean to me? My mother herself was not all that Russian — she left when she was five, after all, and didn't remember much of the language. I enjoyed learning Russian for "O" level, as did my daughter, and got a kick out of singing Tatiana in *Eugene Onegin* in the original Russian — I guess it did feel like a connection. I can still read the Russian characters, even if I don't remember much of the vocabulary. But what I do remember can sometimes come in useful. We once had a Russian builder working in the flat below mine. He had his radio on very loud, so I pushed up my sash window, and shouted: *"Tikho, pozhaluysta"* ("quiet, please"). Astonished, he looked up out of the window, and was shocked into silence!

Growing up, I revelled in the riches of Russian literature: in particular, Tolstoy, Turgenev and the plays of Chekhov. Productions at the Old Vic and National Theatre seemed to bring to life a vision of how the life of my family might have been. Russia felt imbued with an air of romance.

Later in life, there came an unexpected connection between my life and faith and my Russian heritage. Surprisingly, there is a long history of interaction between Quakers and Russia, as recounted in his fascinating book *Friends and Comrades by* Russian Quaker Sergei Nikitin, whom I met in Moscow, and who now lives in England. In 1654, soon after the founding of the Religious Society of Friends (Quakers), one of the founders, George Fox, wrote to Tsar Alexei and when Peter the Great came to England, later in that century, he is known to have visited the Quakers. In the nineteenth century, Tsar Alexander I came to England and attended two Quaker Meetings for Worship.

In the 1890s a number of Quakers made trips to Russia to try to combat the dangers of famine. There was even a mention of Quakers in Pushkin's nineteenth-century novel, *Eugene Onegin*. However, it was in 1916, when my mother was one year old, that the real work of Quakers in Russia began, "prompted by the horrors of the First World War and the flood of refugees streaming into Central Russia from the western borders of the empire" (Nikitin, 13). Four UK Quakers from the mission for refugees went to St Petersburg to provide medical aid and relief for refugees, followed by other groups of medical staff and aid workers from the UK and the USA. In 1918 Quakers opened an orphanage and hospital; circumstances in Russia forced them to leave in 1919, but they were welcomed back a year or so later to help with famine relief. Russia, recognising that they needed help from outside, turned to Quakers, as they had already been to the country, and were a known entity. In 1920 Arthur Watts, a Manchester Quaker, and Anna Haynes, a Quaker from the States, began to distribute food among children's institutions in Moscow. By June 1922, nearly half a million people had been helped by their feeding programme.

For some years in the early 1990s, British Quakers were involved in a Moscow-based project. Then in 1996, some sixty years after the closure of the Quaker centre in Russia, and after extensive international meetings, there began a new international programme involving Quakers from many countries, and a new centre was opened. Since then, Quakers have been deeply involved in many different projects, running reconciliation, mediation and conflict prevention and resolution in many parts of the country.

Since the invasion of Ukraine, Quakers have been hosting a daily international Meeting for Worship to pray for peace in Ukraine. This gathering of Quakers from around the world is so moving, especially in the last ten minutes when we are all invited to put in the chat names of people we'd like to be upheld/prayed for. The names range from individuals and family members to groups of people in Ukraine and elsewhere: "all those working for peace", "all those suffering from homelessness" and so on. A real feeling of kinship.

There are a few worship groups in Russia, mainly in Moscow and St Petersburg. When I and my then partner visited Russia in 2002, we went to Moscow Quaker Meeting, held in a suburb, on the stage of a community hall. It was a small but growing Meeting at the time, with some five members and a number of attenders. Several of them were well acquainted with other European meetings, and one, indeed, is English, a woman who had been spending much of her time working with Chechen refugees in Ingushetiya. She and her colleagues did not then actually go into Chechnya since two volunteers, working partly under Quaker auspices, had been kidnapped and held to ransom a year or so before our visit.

In 2022, I heard that there are two small meetings in Moscow. One meets online every other week with 10–12 attending; the other meets in person with or four or five turning up. One Quaker said to me that maybe the fact that they were so small meant they could still exist. "If the meeting was larger, it may be difficult to find a place to meet. If we were much larger — like thousands — which seems unattainable — we might have problems as a 'sect'. Some groups have problems, others don't. Larger groups and pacifists are more likely to have problems."

When we visited in 2002, as far as we could tell, there were only two Quakers in St Petersburg, and we had supper with one of them, Peter, an English composer, who had got a place at the St Petersburg Conservatoire six years before, and had decided to make it his home: "a big fish", as he put it, "in a small pool". With a long bushy beard, he looked every inch the Russian intellectual, and had obviously established himself well. He had had great problems in getting a residency permit, and was not allowed to earn any money, so he taught a course in British contemporary culture free of charge. His service was, he felt, in sharing the everyday struggles of the Russian people, a struggle that has always saddened me.

Twenty years on, in 2022, I wrote to Peter and discovered that the other Quaker in his Meeting died in 2009. As he is now the only Quaker in St Petersburg, he asked for the meeting to be laid down. Many people have left the city, and a combination of Covid and the current political situation means that Peter, now in his seventies, is quite isolated, but despite the barriers to free speech and the need to "keep under the radar", he continues to love the city, and the "silent majority" of Russians. "I will not be leaving." He has evolved a daily evening prayer routine and finds that the silence on the metro is akin to a Quaker meeting where people centre down internally. It is, he says, a very noisy system so no one tries to talk.

As another Russian Quaker told me, it is in any case hard to meet for worship. Even before the war quite a few draconian laws had been introduced restricting freedom of conscience, including the right of religious groups to gather for worship in premises not officially registered as religious buildings. A situation that echoes the position of the first Quakers in seventeenth-century England.

I was profoundly moved by this voice reaching out from the city of my mother's birth, a new voice echoing so many of the old ones: expressing once again the dichotomy of love for St Petersburg and the hardship of living there.

I knew nothing of these connections with Jews or with Russians when I found a home among Quakers, but, conscious or not, somehow those connections form part of my identity.

The thread of home

Genia lived for the last sixty years of her life in London in a comfortable three-bedroom semi-detached house, a house brimming with Victorian furniture and antiques, much of it inherited from my father's family. After an early life deprived of a permanent home, my mother's surroundings, her possessions, were important to her. The possibility of their loss in the 1950s when my father's illness led to his losing his job must have been particularly traumatic. A friend once told me of a memory she had of standing on a street corner with her mother and suitcases, with nowhere to go. With the memory of fleeing St Petersburg as a small child and arriving penniless on her uncle's and aunt's doorstep in Riga, my mother must have been haunted by the dread of such a fate.

I wonder too whether a faint memory of that family anxiety has led to my own preoccupation with homelessness. When I came to the Quakers in the mid-1990s, the first thing I was asked to do was to co-ordinate the soup runs for homeless people run by various London Quaker meetings. I worked in publishing, had never volunteered, and had no idea about homelessness, so I thought I'd better educate myself. I was shocked at what I found.

On my first soup run, I was nervous: sure that I would either be sneered at as a middle-class do-gooder or hit over the head by a bottle-wielding druggie. Of course neither happened. Instead, as I walked over to a young man in a sleeping bag and asked if he would like a cup of tea or coffee, and whether he took sugar, I found myself forming a relationship with another human being. Instead of passing by a bundle in a doorway with embarrassment and guilt, I was doing something, however small, and my preconceptions fell away. I realised in that moment that

that bundle in the doorway could have been me. And that there is no such thing as "the other". It was an epiphany.

That was the beginning of a continuing concern about homelessness. I live in central London; rough sleepers are my neighbours: I talk to them on a daily basis. In 2010, asking people "What is home to you?" and discovering that it isn't just about shelter — but family, community, hospitality, choice, inner peace — led to writing *Journey Home*, the book, and a few years later to creating a board game of the same name.

And in 2021 to writing *Let Me Take You by the Hand: True Tales of London's Streets*. Although this is about people who work on the streets as well as those who live there, the research led to many interviews with rough sleepers, and hearing their often shocking stories.

We have got used to the sight of people begging on our streets, of bundles in sleeping bags lying in doorways. How have we in a rich country come to accept the fact that people live and often die on our streets? How have we come to this?

* * *

As a small child, living in a comfortable home, I loved nothing more than to escape. Any insecurities about home came later. For me the outside was the real world, the four walls of our flat just a shelter. Apparently my mother was for ever having to run after me as I climbed out of an open window and wandered off. Sometimes, when I was aged about three, she would have to pick up clothes that I had shed along the way.

As I grew up, I followed the traditional pattern of building a career and a family, collecting furniture, often inherited, to furnish our various homes. In Leamington Spa, in London, my husband I enjoyed furnishing our Victorian homes with appropriate and often beautiful furniture.

And then it all changed. As did I. After the break-up of our marriage, I eventually sold the family home and, with my share of the money, bought a flat and an office. In 2001, with a new partner, I went travelling for a year. Afterwards, I wrote:

I found that living out of a rucksack, staying among those with very little, distanced me from the need for many of my possessions and, it seemed, from the need for a permanent "home". It was a strange discovery. Home is such a central part of our "normal" life in the West, and I suppose in most parts of the world. But now that I was alone and did not need to feather a nest for anyone else, the geography of my existence did not seem to be central.

I knew it was likely to be a temporary state but in the meantime was interested to explore the prospect of deliberate homelessness. I knew the restrictions that truly homeless people live with — hard to access a doctor, a dentist, library; excluded from so much that we take for granted — and knew that I was a privileged person: I could give my mother's house for an address should it be needed, and I needed in any case to spend a few days there every month. I was able to make choices.

Not that I was consciously deciding to take this course; it seemed to have grown out of a "not knowing" that I had to obey. The process was becoming a familiar one. Five years before, I had "let go" of my business, my work of some 25 years, without any sense of what I was to do. It led to a complete change in my life. The process of letting go was a startling discovery of a freedom that I vowed would shape the rest of my life. This was the next step.

So I gave my children much of the furniture they grew up with, and a lump sum to help them on the housing ladder. I put everything that I could either online or on direct debit; and put my stuff in storage until I knew that I would not want it. One step at a time. Although I was hitting the road at the time of life that a Hindu becomes a sannyasi, I was not planning to give everything away or become dependent on others. I admired, even envied, the rooted life, but just knew that that was not to be for me, at least for the time being.

Unlike my mother, having benefitted from a secure home as a child, I had no need for the compensation of possessions. I eventually settled into the central London flat that had been my office, with one bedroom, sparsely furnished and fulfilling my main criteria: astonishingly quiet, with a view of the sky. The nomadic impulse has passed, but I still don't find that geography has much to do with my sense of home. Reverting to my three-year-old self, maybe.

My choice of home means that I have forgone the role of *mater familias*. Although I am the oldest female member of the family, I have no room to host big family gatherings, or have more than one person to stay. It is the one thing that I regret: that I have relinquished the role to the next generation, and cannot reciprocate their generosity.

The thread of music

In the midst of the devastation of war and revolution, Dora played the piano. My mother recalled: "She used to play the piano every day for hours and hours — and there was always this music. Chopin and Liszt — they were her favourites." Having studied at the most prestigious conservatoire of the time, why was it that she only gave charity concerts? I wondered if it was a nervous inhibition about performing in public. In which case, I have followed in her path! But, no. It turns out that it was for the same reason that my paternal grandmother had to give up operatic singing when she married. In both countries, it was considered indecorous for a married woman to appear on stage in public.

My mother had other musical memories from her early childhood — of their summer place in Finland, with Dora sitting on some steps down to the lakeside, playing an early version of the musical box. And also of Dora singing to her; in her nineties my mother once sang me a Russian lullaby remembered from that time.

Dora passed on her love of music to her daughter, but not the ear or the aptitude. That skipped generations to me, who trained as a singer and to my daughter, a composer of contemporary classical music. My mother said that Dora had tried to teach her the piano but, like many professionals, she had no patience for teaching her own child. But, even if she couldn't play an instrument and didn't sing, my mother spent a lot of time listening to it, both on the radio and live. She sometimes got tickets for the Royal Opera House from her employers, Rio Tinto Zinc, and, in old age as a partially sighted person, got concessions for seats near the stage. With amusement, she once told a story of being in the front row of the stalls with a friend: "She can't hear and I can't see, but between us...!" In her last decades she got a great deal of pleasure from the live musical evenings hosted at a friend's home.

One story that my mother told us was of an event from her early life, during the family's annual trip to their summer retreat in Finland. My mother had to have been under the age of five at the time, or this might even have taken place before she was born. The picture she painted was of Dora playing the piano in some large bare hall, possibly during a music festival. As she was playing, she noticed a man sitting at the back of the hall. It turned out, so my mother told me, to be the violinist, Fritz Kreisler, who complimented Dora on her playing. It is possible that this was true, that he was there. Kreisler travelled extensively in Europe, including Russia and Scandinavian countries, giving hundreds of concerts, and was at one time apparently smitten with a woman from Finland.

Music has been a powerful thread in my life, woven in from both sides, actually — not only my paternal grandmother but also two of my cousins were or are opera singers, one of whom won Cardiff Singer of the World in 1995. When I was small and supposed to be in bed, my mother and brother would often listen to concerts on the radio. I sat at the top of the stairs, listening, absorbing the music, which has remained a mainstay of my life. I was tempted by the idea of going to music college — in my life it's always been a difficult choice between the literary and the musical — but my mother was adamant about the need to get a university qualification, so it remained a road not taken. Music inhabits me. It is transformative: can change an emotional mood or bring me back to the central core of my spiritual life. As I believe it was for my grandmother, music is the ground of my being.

And singing in particular has always been a joy: from singing nervous solos at primary school, to singing Captain Corcoran in H.M.S. Pinafore in my teens, and lead operatic roles at university. I've had singing lessons from various teachers for much of my life from the age of eighteen till about ten years ago when my Swedish singing teacher no longer came to England. Some years before my mother died, I left my piano at her house: in my small flat there is no room for it, and I don't feel able to make music surrounded by neighbours. But I often wake with a tune in my head. Even in the middle of a sleepless night, I sometimes sing under the bedclothes.

And I feel moved to sing at significant moments. The night before my father died, I sang him "The Lord is my shepherd". And I sang at my son's wedding. When I was first asked to do so, I declined, saying that my nerves would get in the way, but eventually agreed to sing a duet with my daughter. It was a lovely thing to do: I am so glad we did it.

I have always had performance nerves — one reason why I did not make singing a professional part of my life. As I've grown older, I have found a delight in singing in the open air, away from people, feeling at one with the trees, the squirrels who come to watch, and the birds, who I sometimes feel are singing along. About ten years ago I came up with this idea, which is in fact a formalisation of a current practice.

The Hidden Songbird
Wedding, conference, house party, birthday, retreat?
Singing in the landscape.
Hidden, anonymous
Spontaneous, unexpected.
Like an open-air exhibition,
emerging from the shelter
of land and trees
comes a voice.
Whatever the event,
if you have grounds large enough
for a songbird to hide in,
for expenses and a night's

simple board and lodging,
a trained singer offers
a ministry of song

I did a pilot in the gardens of the friend of a friend, which went well, but have never taken it further. But I continue the practice of singing outside, which was particularly important for me during the pandemic when I sang almost daily in Regent's Park. Sometimes people come up to me and express their pleasure: "Thank you so much, it's made my day." But there's no set audience, no expectation. Singing outside, feeling the connection to the natural world, is part of my spiritual practice.

Singing contributes to my wellbeing: it's not surprising that we use the musical terms "in tune", "harmony" to denote a sense of being at ease within ourselves, with others and the whole of creation. Open to Spirit. At peace. People are surprised when I tell them I sing alone. But, even alone, singing is a self-expression, a physical, spiritual and emotional practice that enhances my life.

The Wagner question

My mother loved the music of Wagner.

Like many Germans of his day, Wagner was virulently and unapologetically antisemitic. Hitler was a great admirer of the composer, and a strong link is often made between the two, although Wagner died before Hitler was born. Today his music is banned in Israel.

The Israeli Jewish pianist and conductor, Daniel Barenboim, defends the right to play Wagner's music, and in 2014 conducted the complete Ring Cycle at the BBC Proms,

> Barenboim is ... quick to point out that widespread recognition of Wagner's anti-Semitism did not prevent his music from being performed by Jews even after

Hitler came to power. In Tel Aviv in 1936, for example, the Palestine Philharmonic — precursor to today's Israel Philharmonic — memorably performed the prelude to Act 1 and Act 3 of Lohengrin under the baton of Arturo Toscanini. "Nobody had a word to say about it," Barenboim remarks. "Nobody criticised [Toscanini]; the orchestra was very happy to play it."

A Jewish prohibition on playing Wagner only came into effect later due to what Barenboim describes as the "use, misuse and abuse" of his music by Hitler (https:// www.bbc.com/culture/article/20130509-is-wagners-nazi-stigma-fair)

When I was young, and already in love with classical music, it was the music of Wagner that eluded me. Those vast sweeps of elemental passion and power were hard for a child to understand and assimilate, and it took me time to do so, but gradually the recognisable motifs drew me in.

How, many people would ask, could a woman like my mother whose life was so damaged by the Holocaust, love the music of Wagner, whose antisemitic views, whose influence on Hitler, were so well known? Somehow, though we never discussed it, she was able to separate the two and I have always, although with some discomfort, said that if my mother, my brother and Barenboim can love Wagner's music, it's all right for me. We live in a time when that kind of separation is being questioned. A few days before writing this, there was an attack on the Ariel and Prospero statue outside Broadcasting House in London. The artist, Eric Gill, was known to have abused children, and those attacking the statue felt his art should not be presented in so prominent a place. But that way lies censorship. Somehow people holding revolting views or capable of performing appalling acts can also be the conduit of a sublime creative spirit. When I discussed Wagner with my brother, he agreed.

What is it in Wagner's music that overcomes our distaste at the views of the man who composed it? In his talk on Radio 3 (https://www.bbc.co.uk/sounds/play/m000jp9j),

Tom Service makes a good case for the Ring Cycle being not about promoting Aryan politics, but about love. He says that the song cycle is looking to all of us, the audience, to find a new and better world order. As he says, the "heroes" and gods in the opera all meet a sticky end and maybe we can do better. I can only say that the emotional power of the music in *Lohengrin*, in *Tannhaüser*, in *Tristan und Isolde* and, yes, in the Ring, is overwhelmingly moving.

Threading the needle: unexpected encounters

I

In 1995 I was staying with an actress friend in Gloucestershire, and one morning, as is my wont, I wandered out into the garden and sang. Also staying there was a theatre director, who came out into the garden and said: "I'm directing a play about Chopin and Georges Sand. There's a role for an opera singer. Would you like it?" (The role turned out to be that of Pauline Viardot, friend of Chopin and a composer in her own right.) There followed three weeks of lunchtime performances at the King's Head, Islington. I was working as a literary agent at the time, so at lunchtime I would jump in a cab, change into costume and make-up, perform, change, jump in a cab and go back to work.

II

In 2015 I treated myself to a visit to Cardiff Singer of the World. At a falafel stall outside St David's Hall, I fell into conversation with two women, one of whom turned out to be an accompanist. She lives in France and, hearing that my son also lives there and that I was a singer, she expressed eagerness at making music together. (I was taken aback: usually the eagerness comes from the singer rather than from the accompanist.) In the event, we have met not in France but on her visits to England, usually at the Quaker Meeting House in St Martin's Lane, which the English National Opera use as a regular rehearsal space, and once at my mother's, giving her a little recital a year or so before she died. Gayle turns out to be a voice coach too, and I have never been accompanied by such a magnificent pianist, a woman who urged me to go beyond anything I thought I could do. She was determined to get me to sing in public again and in 2018 she wrote to say that she was working with a young French soprano who wanted to do a recital of duets with a mezzo. Was I interested? Gritting my teeth, I faced my fear of performance and said yes anyway. The other singer and I chose a repertoire — Monteverdi, Purcell, Schumann — and started rehearsing in our separate countries for a concert planned for July 2019. By which time we were in the throes of the pandemic, and so the concert has not taken place.

...and creativity

My mother was a romantic. She told a story of her schooldays, when, daydreaming, she was gazing out of the window. The voice of the teacher brought her back: "Evgenia, what do pigs live off?" Her answer apparently, whether or not she had heard the question, was "Love and fresh air."

If Dora's soul was expressed in music, my mother's spirit came alive in pottery. She attended classes for some years and bought a kiln, which lived in what had originally been an outside lavatory, and was then used in wet weather to dry clothes. Apart from producing the usual kind of pots and bowls, over many years she created a wonderful array of figurines — people and animals, mythical creatures: the mermaids, unicorns and dragons of her romantic imagination. Though, since she could never make the dragons fearsome, they were the source of much mirth. I recently came across a "poem" I'd written some years ago and completely forgotten:

> My mother created a faery world:
>> Unicorns and mermaids,
>> Creatures of myth and a forest law.
>> Yes, dragons, too, but try as she might,
>> She could never make them fierce.
>> There's a softness in the clay,
>> A curve that speaks of gentleness.
>> Baby creatures that never learned to sneer.
>> Suckling on dreams,
>> They were never taught their purpose.
>> Failures, really.
>> Call yourself a dragon!

Some of her figures — a standing violinist, a sitting cellist — expressed her love of music. My daughter sometimes did pottery with her, and in due course inherited the kiln.

The clay figurines were an expression of my mother's romantic imagination, as were the stories that she told us. Inevitably, since hers is the only version of most of the family information that I have, it is hard to know whether the details are exactly true. I needed to take some of them — especially the exploits of her cousin, Lilik, with whom she was half in love, and the virtues of her mother — with a pinch of salt. But her life was indeed dramatic, and although there were, I have no doubt, exaggerations, elaborations, memory embroidered with love-filled wish-fulfilment, most of what she told us was, astonishingly, largely true.

Citizen of the world

My mother firmly rejected any label of refugee or migrant. "I am not a refugee. I came to England because I married Dad." My mother had no memory of feeling at home in Russia. Although in pre-Soviet times, Jews were one of the recognised nationalities in Russia, she experienced it as a place of antisemitism, and only remembered a profound relief at leaving. She never liked Latvia either. It was only when they arrived in Switzerland that she could relax: a place of safety, "a democratic country" for which she had a profound affection and respect. How ironic it was that it was in Switzerland that Lenin had taken refuge; as he came back to Russia, they left.

So it was not so much to Russia that my mother felt allegiance — she left, after all, at the age of five — but to Europe. She related to St Petersburg, that most European of Russian cities, to France, where she went to university and where her cousin lived, and to Switzerland. She felt European. As do I. That feels like my heritage, and I have spent a lot of time and family holidays in various European countries. Like many in the UK, I feel betrayed by Brexit, for our roots as a family are in Europe. At the time, I joked that, although many in my family could maintain their European status by applying for Irish citizenship, the only country apart from the UK that I could claim roots in was Russia, and in these days that doesn't feel a very attractive possibility! The passport I have, with "European Union" on it is still valid, but I am no longer counted as European. At European airports, I have to join the queue for "others"; I no longer belong. A friend of mine from a German Jewish background has taken the courageous step of applying for German citizenship. She feels that this generation of Germans has moved on and that it is time for her to do the same. She did not, however, feel able to tell her mother.

The displacement of my mother's family resulted in it becoming very cosmopolitan. Becca married a Swiss, as did my mother, who then married an Englishman. Mischa married first a Swiss woman and then an Iranian. Berthe married two Frenchmen; her son married a Frenchwoman, a Greek, and then a Guatemalan. You could indeed say that as a family we are citizens of the world!

Not surprisingly, as a child, Genia felt she never had a home; she felt only tolerated in the home of relations. She said that she often felt more at home with friends than her family. "They were good to me. I was happy, we had a lot in common." When she arrived in England in 1945, she was married to an Englishman, so there was no question of her admittance, though it took time for her to settle. She lived in many countries, considered herself adaptable, and embraced different cultures, though some more readily than others.

What, I asked, was her sense of home? "One's own house and home. To be born and brought up in a country that is one's own. Another country is never quite the same." As a foreigner in England, she said she didn't "really feel regarded as part of this country. My loyalties are entirely here, but I have recently felt less at home; it's crept up on me because of all the other nationalities that have come to live here."

There are few people so exercised about the advent of a new wave of refugees as refugees or migrants from a past generation. My mother's last comment sheds a little light on why that is. Those outside a country have a more fixed idea of its identity. I remember the very pronounced ideas about Britain that I came across when travelling around the world. People from other countries were attached to a pastoral idyll where cricket is played on the village lawn, or convinced that London is continually immersed in a Dickensian smog. They did not really want to hear about a rich multicultural community: they wanted their picture of Britain to stay the same as their long-established picture of it.

I think the same may be true of some who settle in this country. On arrival it can take time to settle in: to match the country you arrive in with the country of your imaginings. One young Bulgarian woman I spoke to, steeped in English literature, found it hard to come to terms with the twentieth-century reality. Once established, coming to terms with change may be even more difficult. They know why they have come here, why they wanted this to be their home. Change is not welcome. For someone born here, the (maybe unconscious) sense of belonging is more established. Members of the indigenous population may feel threatened by competition for housing or jobs, but their sense of the identity of the country is less undermined by the advent of people from elsewhere.

The thread of language

pinned on the wall on my aunt's house in Geneva
"On ne peut pas bâtir notre avenir si on perd notre passé"
(We cannot build our future if we lose our past)
— Sebastião Salgado

Linguistic fluency came naturally in my mother's family. It was not a family that spoke Yiddish, but French and German were commonplace, as well as Russian. We don't know what language Dora spoke with her children. She had been born in Latvia, then part of the Russian empire, of course, where German was a common currency, while the educated classes in St Petersburg at that time often spoke French. My mother told me that it was her father who taught her to read and write in Russian. Although apparently half of the city's Jews spoke Russian at home at this time, it would seem from this comment that that was not the case in their home. And family letters from the 1940s seem to have been written interchangeably in French and German. Aunt Becca was a literary translator, from Russian to German.

And speaking more than one language came as second nature in our family too. Both my parents were trilingual, unsurprising in the case of my mother, given her peripatetic history, but more surprising in the case of my father. The English are not renowned for their linguistic prowess. But having spent his early years in South America, my father spoke some Spanish, and seemed to have a talent for languages, picking up Italian, French and German on the way. And he had a love of language itself. I have met few who could equal the wealth of his vocabulary, his knowledge and understanding of language.

My brother Eric's first language was French; when he came back from a year in Palestine, he was speaking German — albeit, he was told, with a Saxon accent. And then, when my parents married, of course he had to learn English. What extraordinary adaptability, to move between languages with such ease. The story goes that when I was small, if Mum and Dad wanted me not to understand, then they would talk French, and if they wanted neither my brother nor me to understand, they spoke German. But of course my brother had been trilingual at the age of five, even if he forgot much of it later, and my mother, a teacher of French and German after all, taught me French at an early age. Nevertheless, it kept us on our toes.

Keeping up the tradition in our more settled place and times, my daughter and I both did "O" level Russian, as well as French and Latin. After university, I followed my mother in doing the Institute of Linguists course in French, though I funked taking the exam. I also did Italian and German; my daughter also did Greek. Sophie, born in 2020, my granddaughter, and Dora's great-great-granddaughter, being brought up in France, will inherit the multi-lingual tradition of, so it turns out, the families of both her parents.

Even after sixty years in England, my mother retained a soft indefinable, perhaps Swiss German, accent. When I was growing up, our family life was peppered with French and German words. *Gemütlich* (cosy); *"tiens"* ("fancy that", "you don't say"); *"je m'en fous"* (polite version: "I couldn't care less"), *"faute de mieux"* ("better than nothing"), and most of all *schimpf* (from the German for to complain), which is still current in family usage. When we were being cheeky, the best phrase was *"et le respect que tu me dois?"* ("and what about the respect you owe me?") Even Russian words popped up. We had a set of luggage, bags which we called *chemodan*, with the little one referred to as *chemodanchik*. Russian is full of diminutives. I affectionately used to call my mother Mammoushka until many years later she told me she found it patronising, and asked me not to. On my visit to my aunt in Geneva, I was amused to discover that her daughter called her Mammoushka too!

There were also jokes based on my mother's early struggles with English pronunciation, as we referred to an umbrella as "wallalla" and pronounced Vaughan Williams as "Worgen Villiams". It was a sign of my mother's grumpiness in old age that when I sat with her on her bed waiting for a carer to take her for a hospital visit and said, "Well, this is rather *gemütlich*, isn't it?" her response was, "I don't think so."

My mother was a writer. She joined a London writers' circle and under various pseudonyms wrote short stories, one of which won first prize in a short story competition in 1954. But English was not her first language, and somehow that showed; had she continued in German, her writing might have been a more important part of her life.

But after the war, she could not bear to read German or to hear it spoken. So, like many refugees, along with the loss of her home and her family was the loss of a language and literature that she loved. With death, murder, genocide came the appropriation of all that the oppressed peoples held dear. So, with what irony in middle age when my father's illness forced her to earn a living to support the family, she had to fall back on the only marketable skill she possessed: her languages. She had her diploma from the Sorbonne, but updated her skills by taking the Institute of Linguists Fellowship exam in French and German before embarking on teaching, which she did for many years: in evening classes at the local institute and at a school for disabled children. And, following her aunt's example, she worked as a translator, in her case from French and German to English at a chemical company. How painful it was for her to return to the language of her youth I can only imagine. Pain and delight, maybe, in equal measure. Guilt and relief.

When she spent a brief spell in hospital not long before she died, imagine the horror when from an elderly woman in the next bed came a stream of abuse — in German. It upset my mother deeply; it may well have been antisemitic, Nazi. Both women were of that era.

But, in general by the time she was old, my mother's love of the language had returned, and she took great pleasure in my singing to her in German in my weekly visits: Schubert, Schumann, music with settings of the beloved poems of her youth. My school German comes in useful but the vocabulary has shrunk to the somewhat limited words of these *lieder*: nightingale, rosebud, stars, love and so on, not a great deal of use for everyday conversation! My piano, of course, had by then taken up occupancy in my mother's house. I've never been able to accompany myself when singing, so my singing was *a capella* except for the occasions when my accompanist came with me — a much richer experience for my mother and myself. He died in the same year as my mother, and with them died most of my opportunities for musical performance.

...and literature

Not only linguistic fluency but a love of literature is a very strong thread in our family.

My mother always referred to Dora's love of not only music but literature. We don't know her literary tastes, except that she owned a very beautiful limited-edition silk-covered Russian edition of Pushkin's *The Queen of Spades*, dated 1917, now in my daughter's possession. Another of the 250 copies is apparently in the Moscow State Museum. Did Dora also read contemporary writers? It seems highly likely. She lived, after all, just after the golden age of Russian literature: Chekhov and Tolstoy were still alive in her lifetime; Dostoevsky died just a few years before she was born. And, later in life, her sister translated some of their works from Russian into German. Following the Russian classics of the Golden Age, their own time in Russia was marked by another peak of artistic achievement, known as the Silver Age (1880s–1917), a period especially renowned for poetry by such writers as Alexander Blok, Anna Akhmatova, and Osip Mandelshtam.

As a linguist, it is likely that Dora would have been familiar with the French and German classics, maybe English too, in translation. Books were expensive, but many, including from foreign authors such as Dickens, Balzac and Victor Hugo, were published in the more affordable literary magazines. The literacy rate in Russia at the time was a a lot lower than in Western Europe, with only those with financial means able to enrol in educational institutions at the secondary and university level. Those who read and even owned books were indeed a privileged educated minority.

A love of literature was something that mother and daughter could share. Growing up in Switzerland, German was Genia's first literary language. She was in love with Heine and Goethe, and later came to know and love French writers such as Proust and Mauriac. She was in her teens when she discovered Shakespeare; she tells of running to her mother with the excitement of the discovery of Sha-kes-pe-a-re!

I inherited that love of literature, read voraciously in English from an early age, as did and does my daughter. I also read a good deal of French literature when studying for "A" level French, and of other literature in translation. I decided to read English literature at university, before going into publishing, and later becoming a writer myself.

The men

In this book, I have traced the threads from only one side of the family. The warp and weft of any human being, with all its rich colour and texture, as well as its threadbare patches, is woven from a number of sources: from the paternal threads as well as the maternal. I am aware that in talking of "threads" it might be assumed that we are talking only of genetic inheritance, DNA, but environmental factors have of course a huge impact on us all. The factors brought to bear through childhood, and to some extent throughout life — parental influence, and that from school, the workplace, and our peers. Nurture as well as nature. As Steven Pinker says:

> [C]oncrete behavioral traits that patently depend on content provided by the home or culture — which language one speaks, which religion one practices, which political party one supports — are not heritable at all. But traits that reflect the underlying talents and temperaments — how proficient with language a person is, how religious, how liberal or conservative — are partially heritable.

It is hard to disentangle such a multitude of threads, and of course I have touched on many of them here. Although this account deliberately prioritises the women of my family, that is not to underestimate the influence of the men.

My mother generally avoided talking about her father, but when she did, she couldn't escape her tendency to romanticise. Apparently, he ran away to join the army at 17 and was captured and imprisoned in the Russo-Japanese War of 1904–1905 — we don't know where, but presumably in Japan. Over 70,000 Russian troops were imprisoned in various cities in Japan, and by all accounts were well treated. It was the first war to be conducted in the context of the Hague Convention's "Laws and customs of war on land" (1899), which includes the requirement that prisoners of war must be humanely treated. Dmitri escaped — so legend has it — with the wife of the commandant. "No," corrected my brother, when I mentioned it, "but with her help, anyway."

Dmitri apparently became a pharmacist and made a lot of money from patents — was obviously a good businessman — but when the First World War broke out, he was called up. He became an officer (possibly his downfall) and decorated. He was one of many Jews to be involved. Although Jews were accused of German sympathies during the war, apparently over half a million Jews served in the tsarist army. Nonetheless, the Russian government refused to modify their anti-Jewish policies. It was not until the Revolution that things changed.

We may know little of Dmitri's life, but his legacy remains in the scientific bent to be seen in his descendants. His son Mischa was a geneticist. In 1946, he received a Ph.D. from the University of Zurich. After a year of postdoctoral research at the University of Basel, he went to the Institute of Animal Genetics in Edinburgh on a two-year research fellowship. He became Jenkinson Memorial Lecturer in Embryology and head of the Embryology Laboratory at Oxford in 1951. In 1961 he was a visiting professor at the Rockefeller Institute and in 1961 was appointed Professor and took the direction of the Station of Zoology and of the Laboratory of General Zoology (university of Geneva). On his death in 1998, there were full-page obituaries in the Swiss press.

Dmitri's scientific bent passed not only to his son, but to Mischa's own children: Jean-François, a specialist in Bio Field Information Technology and Owner, BFit Labs slu; and his younger sister, Scheherazade, who became a doctor. And on my mother's side, the thread continued with my brother Eric, who studied and for many years taught biology and his son, a microbiologist.

Of the other men in previous generations of the family I know little, except Genia's mother's brother, Uncle Sasha, a rather touching figure, who apparently paid for her and her brother's education. As a Jew, he was forbidden to work in his original profession of engineer, so he became a pharmacist and, as a bachelor, could afford to help out when Dora, by then divorced, had had to leave everything behind.

Growing up, I heard next to nothing about the others: Becca's husband Franz, nor that of my mother's cousin Berthe, though she herself was quite a presence in our lives.

My brother said that my mother didn't like men very much. Was that true? It is certainly the case that she didn't talk of them much, but if the men seem to play a smaller part in this story, it is because in some ways they excluded themselves.

Absence

If Dora was a strong presence in my life, my grandfather, Dmitri, was noted for his absence. He barely existed. My mother would rarely talk of him, and there was no picture of him in the house, nothing to remind her of her father or tell us about our grandfather. I felt sad, frustrated, not to know anything of him, and in 1998, when the daughter of a Holocaust survivor gave me the name of an organisation that might be able to help, I came quite close to trying to find out. I felt I owed it to him to know, to shed the blinkers of my youth and find out the truth about my Jewish family. But I needed to get some more facts from my mother, and I deferred the moment. The following year, travelling in Poland as part of a travelling scholarship, I got a little lost and came across a bleak memorial in Polish, Yiddish and English: "Along this road 300,000 Jews were driven to the extermination camps."

That, and the discovery that my hotel was on the site of the Warsaw ghetto, was a shocking reminder of my quest, what a friend refers to as a cosmic nudge, a spiritual shove between the shoulders. I did get as far as doing the recorded interview with my mother and wrote a piece for the Quaker magazine about my resolve, but was still hesitant and failed to take the next step. It was only after my mother's death that my nephew tracked down on the internet a picture of my grandfather from a passport issued in Riga in 1929. Dmitri would have been about forty. A handsome, smartly dressed, dark-haired man with strong dark brows, he looked remarkably like my nephew. And we discovered his real name. But who was this man? My mother remembered so little of him, and was almost successful in erasing him from history.

The absence of her father had a profound impact on Genia. It is, perhaps, meaningful that she married, as she put it, "two sick men". One who died young, and the other who in his illness was absent much of the time, sometimes in person but more often in his sense of self.

And in my own life, the Holocaust was not the only shadow as I grew up: the other was my father's mental illness.

1950s: A psychiatric hospital. Shadowy figures, grey ghosts wandering the corridors, my father one of them, indistinguishable. It was a traumatic experience for a child, and I never repeated it. In fact, my father never wanted me to see him there. A brilliant man, he broke down in his thirties and throughout my childhood was often drugged, in and out of sanity, in and out of hospital. Absent from our home, from himself, and, often in a parallel world, from me. He could not be reached. But that was not the case all the time. He was often enough his remarkable self for me to know I do not want him to join that army of ghosts already haunting my life. He was real. He was my dad, I loved him and I always knew he loved me.

But he was hard to live with. His illness was controlled by drugs, but so was he; an agonising seesaw for years between his independence and the family being able to cope. He suffered from religious delusions, which led him to talk to himself almost continuously, and make signs of the cross to people in the street. More extremely, the voices that he heard persuaded him on one occasion to take a suitcase of money out of the bank and empty it into the gutter and, in an act of mortification of the flesh, to pour boiling water over his arm, resulting in numerous skin grafts. One unforgettable night, when I was in my teens, I sensed him slipping into delusion — I had become adept at recognising the signs. We had a powerful discussion during which I felt I was hanging on to my own sanity, struggling to remember that the madness was in him not me. It felt like a mediaeval mystery play, with the angel on one shoulder, an evil spirit on the other.

And those absences experienced in childhood continued into the next generation. A much-loved and loving husband and father was not always there either, when drink took a hold, an absence horribly reminiscent of my father's mental illness. And in the end, after twenty-two years, my husband left. After the break-up of my marriage, in therapy the connection was made when the therapist asked me: "What is your father's illness to you?"

"A big black cloud."

"Draw it."

And I did so, grounding the trauma, bringing some healing to my childhood and adult self.

Maybe it is the theme of absence in my life, and in the lives of other women in my family, that renders some of Wagner's music almost unbearably potent. Wotan's farewell to his much-loved daughter Brünnhilde in *Die Walküre* is so moving that there have been times in my life when I find it too painful to hear. It expresses the profound love of a father for his daughter, and the pain of his parting reminds us all of the pain of absence.

Sometimes it is hard to know if a darker perspective on the world comes from intergenerational trauma, or more immediate familial circumstances. All I can say is that any dark times in my life have been rare. In general I have been blessed with an optimistic disposition, heightened by love from family and friends and the privilege of finding self-expression in my work.

* * *

Genia's two husbands may have been "sick", as she said, but were also highly intelligent interesting men, with whom she had a lot in common.

And there were also other, strong, male presences in Genia's life: her brother Mikhaïl (Mischa) and her cousin Alec (Lilik). She loved them both and saw them often when circumstances allowed. We saw a good deal of Mischa during the 1950s. We all went to stay him in Edinburgh when he was there, and often visited him later when he was at Oxford — I remember arguing with him about animal experimentation. When my parents and I were in Malaya, my brother stayed with him during the school holidays. Later on, my mother and I visited him in Geneva. He was very present in our lives.

We also saw a little of my mother's adored cousin, Lilik, when he came over to visit, and stayed with him both in Brussels when I was a child and, many years later, in Guatemala. We were very fond of his third wife, Christy, and continued to see her after Lilik's death. In our year-long travels, my then partner Stephen and I stayed with her in their lovely house in Antigua, Guatemala, and my mother and daughter flew out to join us.

Lilik, born in 1918, was the same age as Mischa (and coincidentally as my father), and at the outbreak of war was a young medical student in Paris. In his book *No Drums, No*

Trumpets, he relates his experiences as a soldier in campaigns in France, Tunisia, Egypt and Germany as he pursued his ambition to join the Free French. He was captured four times and he escaped four times — once from the Sachsenhausen concentration camp — and lost his spleen after being tortured by the Gestapo. On reaching neutral territory, he was seconded to a unit of the Resistance harrying the German forces that were occupying France and in the weeks following D-Day Alec was appointed commander of an area of south-west France. He was finally demobbed in 1945 as Captain in the Marines paratroop commandos and was awarded fourteen decorations including the Croix de Guerre. He was a romantic figure to us all with, as my mother put it, a toothbrush in every port. Married three times, first of all to the daughter of a Frenchman who sheltered him in the war, and finally to the love of his life, Christy, a Guatemalan with whom he spent many happy years, first in France, then in Guatemala, until his death in 1997.

Capture and escape: the theme of the lives of so many in this story. Unlike others, Lilik escaped each time. Unlike them, his capture did not end in death, and he lived literally to tell the tale.

England: The last years

My mother was an extraordinarily resilient woman. Despite an artistic, romantic nature, and a deceptively gentle air, she had an inner strength that enabled her to cope with the terrible death of her family, the loss of her first husband and many years of coping with my father's illness, and the need to provide for her family. She never sought counselling help, probably never saw the need for it, though intergenerational trauma could well have been a reality. She enjoyed many aspects of life, and sought succour in friendship, the Kabbalah and her artistic activities.

After a lifetime of generally good health, in her seventies my mother's eyesight began to fail. A combination of glaucoma and macular degeneration eventually deprived her of reading, one of her most cherished activities. After a lifetime of grief and loss, this gradual loss of sight was at last something that she found unbearable. She became partially sighted, unable to recognise faces, and would pronounce on an almost daily basis: "I'm blind, you know."

My mother was not at her best in old age. She was tired of life — and it had been a long and challenging one. She became self-absorbed, bad-tempered and at times confused. She said she had lost her faith. Earlier in her life she took comfort in the thought that in the afterlife she would meet her mother, my father and others she had loved. It was so sad to think that that consolation had now left her. However, while writing this book I was cheered to hear from my mother's pharmacist, one of the people closest to her in her last years, that right at the end of her life my mother had reported "seeing" Dora, that when she was on the verge of sleep, her mother had come to her. She felt Dora was calling her. After a lifetime of thinking of, praying for, her mother, just before her own death, Genia felt the response, a tug on the ancestral thread.

And at times my mother would rally, and her essence shone through. This, from December 2015, at the age of 100 is, although edited by her grandson, Alex, and not verbatim, a remarkable pronouncement:

> People have asked me what my philosophy of life is. It is really simple. Beauty is a state where everything is present in perfect balance. Therefore all one has to do in life is to expand the beauty in each situation and then our relationships and surroundings will become more beautiful and our lives more beautiful too. This applies to what we do, what we say and what we think and to each and every way we express ourselves. There are no problems that cannot be solved with beauty. God is invisible because he is beyond existence but his footprints consist of beauty therefore we can be certain that he is there and by increasing beauty we are carrying out his will and in so doing becoming closer to him. (Genia Hanrott, edited by Alex Weil, Dec. 2015)

Beauty: such a hallmark of her life, in her person, in her pottery, and in her home. And, as far as we can gather, it was so for her mother too, in her life and music. An antidote to the pain and suffering faced by them both.

And in extreme old age, Genia's spirit was still very much alive. When she reached her hundredth birthday, she told me: "I had a call from the palace, saying they wanted to arrange a time to bring me a letter from the Queen." My nephew took up the story:

> She said: "I don't want it." There was a pause, then they said, "People usually do. We are thinking of coming on Wednesday."
>
> "Oh, that's no good. I've got an appointment with the chiropodist."

Age sometimes seems to endow us with a freedom from the need to please!

To celebrate her hundred years, we gave a party at her house, attended by friends and family, including her beloved sister-in-law and niece from Geneva. On the wall was a collection of photos of her from babyhood to the present day. I gave a little speech, and asked if she had anything to say. After a little reflection, she said: "Love."

Genia lived to an age almost twice that at which her own mother died. She died in March 2017, at the age of 102 in the house she had lived in for over sixty years, a house coincidentally built in the year of her birth. Her death was unexpected. She was not ill. Frailer, certainly, wandering a little in her mind, fitted with a pacemaker by then, but had few medicaments. She had simply had enough. She chose — and I think it was a choice — to die alone. My nephew had gone for a walk, her carer was in another room, and I, I was in America at a conference. I had travelled obstinately, as I often do, without a computer, my only means of contact an old Nokia phone, which unexpectedly, and for the first time in my experience, had the wrong SIM card. After a few days of frustration, failing to establish my ID in order to access emails on another computer, I eventually got through. Saying "I'd better check, just in case my mother has dropped dead". And she had. Just dropped where she sat in her sitting room. Alone. No family reunion around her bedside, no poignant last words, just a silent relinquishing. Hearing the news in that way was, of course, a terrible shock — I think I went white — but I was among kind people, who gave me the space to come to terms with what had happened before coming home to deal with what needed to be done.

Funeral 3 April 2017

We had had plenty of time over the years to discuss what my mother wanted. A few months before her death, she expressed her wishes for a secular service with poetry and music, cremation, and ashes scattered in the crematorium gardens. The place where my father and so many of her friends ended up. So there was to be no headstone, but we considered putting something in the Book of Remembrance as we had done with my father. We also thought of paying for a seat in the Royal Opera House — a place that she loved — to be named for her.

I was saddened, surprised that my mother chose to have a secular funeral. She was a Jew, not practising, certainly, but an adherent of the Kabbalah, the ancient Judaic mystic tradition that meant so much to her in the later part of her life. Golders Green Crematorium was not a place I would have chosen for a meaningful ceremony, but we tried to make it so. We decided to do the service ourselves, not feeling that we needed the intervention of someone who hadn't known my mother.

Our voices were punctuated by brief times of silence so that we could all think of our memories in whatever way we wished. In his newly learned Hebrew, my brother read out the Kaddish, the Jewish prayers for the dead. Her grandson, Alex, feeling he had served her in life, chose not to contribute. Her other grandchildren, my children, each read a poem, and I gave a eulogy.

When I chose the music for the funeral, Dora's presence was very much to the fore. Knowing that my mother's earliest memories were of her mother playing the piano, and my grandmother's love particularly for Chopin and Liszt, I chose a Chopin nocturne, op 9 no. 1. For the second piece, as we processed out of the crematorium, I chose a piece beloved by my mother, the *Pilgerchor* from Wagner's *Tannhaüser*. In doing so, I was again joining up the threads. If Chopin was about the living Dora, Wagner was indirectly about her death. My grandmother's presence now seemed not only appropriate but a crucial reminder of that most vital "thread of life".

If friends and family left the funeral with Dora-inspired music ringing in their ears, after refreshments at my mother's house, they left with tangible reminders of the spirit of my mother. Each carried away a bubble-wrapped figurine — a mother and child, a drunk on a bench, a violinist — or a plaque: a moonlit woodland scene, St George and the dragon, the lady and the unicorn. As she had wished, my mother's ashes were scattered over the garden of the Golders Green crematorium, to join those of my father and of many of their friends.

In my eulogy, I traced her life journey from St Petersburg to Riga, to Switzerland, to Egypt, and finally to England. I said:

The last few years were not easy for Mum. She was tired, wanting to go. We talked about death from time to time, and she would say: "But it's just not happening, is it?" In the end, she retreated and was reluctant to speak. It was easy for those who loved her to lose sight of how things had been. For me, I remember a mother to whom I could always pick up the phone, who always wanted to know that I was safe when I had been on a trip, who was always interested in what I was doing and always read my books. Someone with whom I could share a confidence or a giggle. Who brought me up to care about people, to love the arts and, in later life someone who shared my sense of faith.

I could think of no better tribute than what she had chosen to have put in the Book of Remembrance for my father: "A remarkable human being".

The thread of history

War and Peace

Although I had loved Tolstoy's *Anna Karenina* for many years, I didn't get around to reading his magnum opus, *War and Peace*, until 2001, when a journey around the world included a week on the trans-Siberian Express. It seemed an entirely appropriate place to come to terms with its length, and all those names! And so it proved to be.

The history of Russia, as for many countries, is a history of war. In February 2022 when Russia's invasion of Ukraine caused me to take a pause in writing this book to assimilate what had happened, I realised that it was simply another chapter in that history. However forbidden the use of the word currently is in Russia, this is yet another war. War after war: the Russo-Japanese War, the First World War, the Russian Civil War, the Second World War. What an impact on the country and for its people.

With hindsight, even poet Nina Berberova saw the October Revolution in which she had initially been an eager participant in a different light.

> The Revolution was not inevitable. The twentieth century has taught us that poverty and inequality, exploitation and unemployment are overcome in different ways ... Only underdeveloped countries have revolutions ... while developed countries manage change *differently*. (81)

During the Second World War, Berberova was in exile in Paris watching events in Russia from afar, and recording them as they unfolded, in her powerful "Black Diary". Having lived through the Russian Revolution and civil war, she felt the reverberations through the ages. As the bombs fell in Paris, as the Germans marched into Russia, there was a powerful sense of *déjà vu*. The bombings, the starvation, the arrests, the murders: in parallel in the present and juxtaposed on the past. Berberova had her finger on the pulse not only of the émigré community, but of a whole generation living through repeated loss of life and violations of liberty.

> The entire past is with me. It exists simultaneously with the present (443).

But what about my own family? Her Story? Was the story of Dora, or Genia, one of war? My mother didn't talk about peace. She backed Israel in the six-day war, and continued to promote its cause against the Palestinians. We cannot know about Dora, but, given her reportedly gentle and artistic nature, I don't see acceptance of war as part of her identity. In writing this book, I have not wanted the only memory of Dora to be one of her as a victim, defeated by the ugliness of war. I wanted to celebrate the life of a remarkable, gifted and spiritual woman who left us a rich and multi-faceted legacy.

And My Story? For thirteen years I facilitated workshops for Alternatives to Violence Project (AVP), a conflict management programme, and learned so much from others, including those in prison, about how to deal with conflict nonviolently. Having been blessed with the absence of war in my own life, maybe growing up in the shadow of one with all its appalling consequences, had an unconscious impact. Although I've never been tested, I've always felt strongly about the absolute importance of "Thou shalt not kill" (or, as the Hebrew actually says, "commit murder"): that nothing justifies the taking of a life, whether as a state punishment or personal retribution. Earlier in the book I asked "Why antisemitism?" In a similar rather Emperor's New Clothes kind of way, I find myself asking

"Why violence?" Yes, fear; yes, power struggles. Yes, in-the-moment instinctive violence, perhaps. But calculating, planned, long-term violence — war? When has it ever succeeded? How is it that we never learn that violence begets more of it, that it never works. All that pain, suffering, all those deaths. In the First World War, all those lives lost to gain inches of ground. Why?

BBC Russia editor, Steve Rosenberg, has seen his share of conflict. Having spent nearly the whole of his adult life in Russia, he has seen the country's double-headed eagle face first one way and then the other: swinging from East to West like a metronome; open, then closed. In 2023, he spoke on Radio 3's Private Passions about his life in the country that he regards as home. Like my mother in her credo, beauty is at the core of what he has to say. "This country that has produced such beauty … I hope, I really, really hope … that what is beautiful about Russia once again comes to dominate, and to decide the future of this country."

This story is one of contrasts: the beauty of St Petersburg and the brutality which took place within its walls; the gentle beauty of Dora and the atrocity of her treatment. A story that gives glimpses of the paradoxes of the human spirit: the ugliness and beauty of which humanity is capable; how imagination can be used to calculate ways to torture and to kill — or how it can be used to create beauty; how it can tune in to the music of the spheres.

Epilogue

It was time to say a final farewell to my childhood home. My mother, who had lived there for over sixty years, and whom I had visited weekly for the past thirty years or so, had died the year before, and we were selling the house. It's a spacious suburban London semi that my mother had made a centre for family gatherings, and some years ago, when we were between homes of our own, my children and I spent a few weeks living there.

The house had now been stripped of anything memorable. On a previous visit, I had walked through the empty rooms, sending blessings and peace, but that morning I was just there to let in the clearance men from the homeless charity, Emmaus, who were going to take the few last bits and pieces from the house, and empty the shed. So, on that morning, there was nothing for me to do except sit on the stairs and listen to the comings and goings of the clearance men, and the murmurings of the new owner and his architect who turned up later to discuss their plans.

Feeling somewhat forlorn, I went out into the sunshine of the front garden, and saw a young man studying the Emmaus van, and taking down the details. I said hello, and he asked if I knew anything about the van. I explained that we were clearing my mother's house. He asked me about her, and I gave a brief account of the hundred and two years of her life. What an extraordinary century it had been; how, leaving St Petersburg in 1920, she had escaped the aftermath of the Russian Revolution; how many of her family had died in the Holocaust. He listened attentively, then after a pause said: "I wish you only happy memories of your mother", then: "Remember, that if someone lives such a long life, they have outlived all the evil deeds."

Sunshine. Stillness. We shook hands and, my farewells done, I turned and walked away, feeling completely at peace.

One of my favourite films is *Wings of Desire*, in which a guardian angel wants to become a human being — wants the love, the feelings, the suffering as well as the joy. We first realise that Damiel is no longer an angel when we see his footprint: a palpable sign of embodiment, of being a human being, with all the frailty and glory that that entails.

That day I felt as if I had seen the footprint. I felt as if an angel had crossed my path.

Chronology

(not always clear which calendar is being used)
1855 Paulina Behumann (later Aronson) b Riga
1884 Dora Aronson, b Riga
1885 Dmitri Zamuels (Moshe Shmul) Fishberg b Mohilev, Ukraine
1896 Felix Weil b Rathenau, Germany
1904–05 Dmitri POW in Russo-Japanese War
1914, 3 February: Dora and Dmitri marry in St Petersburg
1915, 6 January: Evgenia (Genia) Fischberg b St Petersburg
1918 Michaïl (Mischa) Fischberg b St Petersburg
    Eric Hanrott b London
1920 Dora, Genia and Mischa leave St Petersburg and arrive in Riga
1922 Dora and Genia leave Riga and arrive in Switzerland
1936 Genia m Felix Weil
1939 Eric Weil b Cairo
1940 Genia and little Eric visit Riga
1941 Dora, Sascha and their mother, Paulina, are killed in Riga.
    Dmitri is killed in Riga
    Felix dies in Palestine
1943 Genia m Eric Hanrott
1947 Jennifer Hanrott b London
1986 Eric Hanrott dies
1988 Mischa dies
2017 Genia dies.

Further reading

Anders, Isabel, *Spinning Straw, Weaving Gold*. Circle Books, 2012

Ayrton, Pete (ed.), *Revolution! Writing from Russia 1917*. Chelmsford: Harbour Press, 2017

Berberova, Nina, trans. Philippe Radley, *The Italics are Mine*. London: Chatto & Windus, 1990

Bruyneel, Sally, *Margaret Fell and the End of Time: The Theology of the Mother of Quakerism*. TX: Baylor University Press, 2010

Budnitskii, Oleg, *Russian Jews Between the Reds and the Whites, 1917–1920*. PA: University of Pennsylvania Press, 2012

Christie, Agatha, *Elephants Can Remember*. London: Harper, 2002.

Cooper, Artemis, *Cairo in the War 1939–1945*. London: Hamish Hamilton, 1989

Dreizin, Felix, *The Russian Soul and the Jew*. Maryland: University Press of America, 1990

Endstad, Johannes D, *Soviet Russians under Nazi Occupation*. Cambridge: CUP 2018

Ezergailis, Andrew *The Holocaust in Latvia, 1941–1944*. Historical Institute of Latvia, Riga; United States Holocaust Memorial Museum; Washington, DC, 1996

Gillman. Harvey, *A Minority of One*. London: Quaker Home Service, 1988

Hodgkin, Joanna *Amateurs in Eden*. London: Virago, 2012.

Laqueur, Walter, *The Changing Face of Antisemitism*. Oxford University Press, 2006

Le Vernoy, Alec, *Without Drums or Trumpets*. London: Sphere, 1990

McAuley, Mary, *Bread and Justice: State and Society in Petrograd 1917–1922*. Clarendon Press, 1991

McGeever, Brendan, *Antisemitism in the Russian Revolution*. Cambridge: CUP, 2019

Michelson, Frida and Goodman, Wolf, *I Survived Rumbuli*. New York: Holocaust Library, 1979 [Rumbuli is the alternative name for Rumbala. They seem to be used interchangeably.]

Nikitin, Sergei, trans. Suzanne Eade Roberts, *Friends and Comrades*. York: Quacks books, 2022

Pinker, Steven, "Why nature & nurture won't go away". Daedalus. volume 133, issue 4, Fall 2004

Polonsky, Antony, *The Jews in Poland and Russia*, Volume 3: 1914–2008. Littman Library of Jewish Civilization, 2011

The Jews in Poland and Russia: a short history,

Reed, John, *Ten Days that Shook the World*. London: Penguin, 1977

https://www.bbc.com/culture/article/20130509-is-wagners-nazi-stigma-fair

Sherman, A.J., *Mandate Days: British Lives in Palestine, 1918–1948*. MA: The John Hopkins Press, 2001.

https://yivoencyclopedia.org/article.aspx/riga)

The author

Jennifer Kavanagh worked in publishing for nearly thirty years, the last fourteen as an independent literary agent. In the past twenty years, she has run a community centre in London's East End, worked with street homeless people and refugees, and set up microcredit programmes in London, and Africa. She has also worked as a research associate for the Prison Reform Trust.

Jennifer now spends most of her time writing, speaking, and running retreats. She has published eleven previous books of non-fiction and three novels. She is an associate tutor at Woodbrooke Quaker study centre, a Churchill Fellow, a Fellow of the Royal Society of Arts and a member of a community of fools. She lives in London, England.

Liberalis is a Latin word which evokes ideas of freedom, liberality, generosity of spirit, dignity, honour, books, the liberal arts education tradition and the work of the Greek grammarian and storyteller Antoninus Liberalis. We seek to combine all these inter-linked aspects in the books we publish.

We bring classical ways of thinking and learning in touch with traditional storytelling and the latest thinking in terms of educational research and pedagogy in an approach that combines the best of the old with the best of the new.

As classical education publishers, our books are designed to appeal to readers across the globe who are interested in expanding their minds in the quest of knowledge. We cater for primary, secondary and higher education markets, homeschoolers, parents and members of the general public who have a love of ongoing learning.

If you have a proposal that you think would be of interest to Liberalis, submit your inquiry in the first instance via the website: www.liberalisbooks.com.